Twayne's United States Authors Series

Upton Sinclair

TUSAS 294

Upton Sinclair

UPTON SINCLAIR

By WILLIAM A. BLOODWORTH, JR.
East Carolina University

TWAYNE PUBLISHERS
A DIVISION OF G. K. HALL & CO., BOSTON

Library of Congress Cataloging in Publication Data

Bloodworth, William A
  Upton Sinclair.

  (Twayne's United States authors series; TUSAS 294)
  Bibliography: p.169 - 73
  Includes index.
  1. Sinclair, Upton Beall, 1878-1968—Criticism and interpretation.
PS3537.I85Z572   813'.5'2   77-24754
ISBN 0-8057-7197-2

PRINTING   6 7 8 9 YEAR   3 4 5

To my parents

Contents

About the Author

William Bloodworth is an Associate Professor of English at East Carolina University, where he teaches courses in American literature. His study of Sinclair and the problems of American literary radicalism is part of a larger interest in how American writers have attempted to deal with social problems.

A native of San Antonio, Texas, Professor Bloodworth holds degrees in English from Texas Lutheran College and Lamar University. At the University of Texas he earned the Ph.D. in American Civilization and became interested in the Progressive Era in general and Upton Sinclair in particular. He is currently at work on studies of other literary figures of the same period and on studies of Western American literature.

Preface

This book is a narrative of the career of the writer who is best known for having turned the stomach of a nation. Upton Sinclair burst upon the American literary scene in 1906 when *The Jungle* told readers exactly what it was like to work in a packing plant, exactly what kind of filthy processes were involved in the packing of meat, and exactly how corrupt the whole meat packing industry was. Sinclair was more than a muckraker, and *The Jungle* was more than an attempt to tell "exactly how" things were, but the images persist. In my treatment of Sinclair I have not tried to change these images but to expand them, to enlarge our understanding of Sinclair and his efforts as a writer.

Sinclair's literary efforts, spanning seven decades of American life, were prolific. Born in 1878, Sinclair made his first marks in the literary world by authoring hundreds of adventure stories for boys in the late 1890's. From this auspiciously commercial beginning he went on to develop an idealistic vision of the artist's responsibility to oppose materialism and injustice. In the early years of the twentieth century this vision led him to Socialism and to the writing of *The Jungle*. After *The Jungle* Sinclair continued his feud against social and economic injustice for nearly sixty years. By the time of his death in 1968 he had published nearly fifty novels, more than twenty books of nonfiction, several plays, hundreds of pamphlets, and thousands of articles, editorials, and letters. These works touch on aspects of modern life ranging from politics to diet, from venereal disease to extrasensory perception. Sinclair's involvement with political and social concerns, including his nearly successful campaign for governor of California in 1934, was greater than that of any other twentieth century American writer.

But we can approach no writer in mere quantitative terms. Sinclair has always been something of a controversial figure in American letters. Sympathetic critics have generally seen him as a passionate crusader who selflessly attacked injustice whenever it reared its ugly head in American life and who shied away from few subjects, however unpopular they were at the time. Alfred Kazin's 1942 estimate of Sinclair as "a touching and curious symbol of a certain old-fashioned idealism" yet also "one of the forces leading to the modern spirit in America" is a typical sympathetic evaluation.[1] Among foreign readers, Sinclair has been almost as popular as Jack London, his friend and contemporary. On the other hand, detractors have always found Sinclair an easy target. Politically, he is not only open to attacks from conservative critics, but his liberal ideas are often inconsistent, his radicalism often naive. His support of such quackish causes as fasting and psychic healing has often been an embarrassment to readers who might agree with him politically. Recent radical critics, those with a New Left orientation, have found little inspiration in Sinclair. Above all, he has been scorned by literary critics and scholars who find him simple-minded and shallow beside the great twentieth century writers who were, after all, his competitors in the race for reputation and recognition.

Although what I have to say about Sinclair is both critical and appreciative, I have rather consciously tried to slant my discussion in the direction of understanding and explanation, not attack or defense. Specifically, I have tried to trace his writing career from its juvenile origins to its last expressions and, in so doing, to show its interrelationship with his life and his times. Furthermore, since Sinclair considered his most important literary role to be that of a novelist, I have devoted considerable attention to his best works of fiction—*The Jungle, King Coal, Oil!,* and *Boston.*

Throughout, I have tried to keep in mind what I think is his primary place in American literary and social history—as an energetic, persistent, and generally articulate voice of pre-World War I reform. He matured during the Progressive Era, became famous as a muckraking novelist and reformer, and seldom strayed far, or for very long, from his role as a propagandist for social justice. His Socialism was often more thoroughgoing and critical than the progressive positions of other spokesmen for the period, but it was always reformistic rather than revolutionary, always aimed at correcting abuses through established democratic means. His expressions were also youthfully enthusiastic and earnest, even when the Progressive Era was no more than a memory, and Sinclair himself was far from young. Continually, in the histories of his times, Sinclair is described in the terms of youth. Louis Filler says that "Sinclair was a boy—a desperately earnest one, with a head filled with dreams and fancies."[2]

Howard Mumford Jones refers to him as "a young political idealist."[3] Alfred Kazin speaks of *The Jungle* as "the story of the betrayal of youth by the America it had greeted so eagerly."[4] Youthful, earnest, adolescent, innocent—these are not only Sinclair's qualities but, in many respects, also the outward and visible features of his era. Because he made serious literature of these qualities, particularly through the medium of what he called the "contemporary historical novel," no picture of twentieth century American literary life could pretend to be complete without him.

I have also tried to emphasize two points about Sinclair's writings, particularly his novels. The first is that he wrote fiction which was primarily outward in direction and horizontal in scope. He was concerned mainly with the exterior world of society, economics, and politics. He was specifically concerned in many of his books with the facts and problems of working-class life. In general, he struggled to present things as they were and as they could be documented by facts and evidence. Almost always his fiction was based on notes, interviews, and observations of his subject. He strove for this kind of objectivity because he wished to convince his readers of the true nature of a world that he felt they could change. This world—not the world of words that the artist created, and not the complex world of consciousness and unconsciousness—was his muse and his adversary.

The second point may defy the first. My discussion of individual works, as well as my overall narrative of Sinclair's career, repeatedly points to the thematic conflict of an idealist struggling against various social forces. This conflict shaped Sinclair's life and provided him with literary work for more than half a century. In its simplest pattern, the conflict involves the idealistic sensibility unified against an obviously unjust capitalist society. This pattern is the one projected by Sinclair's often announced role as a crusader for social justice. At its most complex, the conflict takes the form of an idealist who is not only opposed to an unjust society but also at odds with his or her own social responsibilities, family loyalties, or deeply en-grained cultural responses. This pattern runs throughout Sinclair's early life and finds expression in much of his fiction. Often it results in a "genteel radical" sensibility combining traditional nurture and values with radical political leanings. This sensibility identifies both the person who wrote *The Jungle* and its narrative voice. It also identifies the divisions within the central characters of later achievements like *Oil!* and *Boston.*

My first two chapters are weighted with biography because Sinclair's later works were strongly influenced by his early years. The child seems especially to have been the father of the man. In these two chapters, early and seldom-read works are also dealt with at some length in order to document the religious, literary, and political development of Sinclair's temperament and thought. Later chapters deal more sparingly with biography and minor works.

I willingly take credit for the limitations of this book and offer my gratitude to those whose assistance has helped make possible its insights. To Robert M. Crunden of the American Civilization Program at the University of Texas I owe long standing and deeply felt intellectual debts. The staff of the Lilly Library at Indiana University graciously assisted me in examining the Sinclair Archives. David Sinclair has allowed me permission to make use of his father's published and unpublished works. Completion of my manuscript was made possible by the English Department of East Carolina University, which has given me clerical assistance and released time from teaching duties. To Julia and Nicole—and to Paul, too—I owe immeasurable debts of time, patience, and love.

WILLIAM A. BLOODWORTH, JR.

Greenville, North Carolina

Chronology

Party because he disagrees with its antiwar philosophy.

1918–1919 Writes and publishes *Upton Sinclair's*, a monthly magazine. Also begins to publish his own books in Pasadena.

1927 *Oil!* published.

1928 *Boston* published.

1932 *American Outpost*, an autobiography, published.

1934 Sinclair wins the Democratic primary for governor in California but is narrowly defeated in the general election.

1940 Begins writing the Lanny Budd series, publishes *World's End*.

1949 Publishes the tenth Lanny Budd novel, *O Shepherd, Speak*.

1959 Mary Craig Sinclair publishes *A Southern Belle*, her autobiography, as she suffers from a fatal heart disease.

1961 Mary Craig dies.

1962 Sinclair marries May Hard. *The Autobiography of Upton Sinclair* published.

1968 Sinclair dies at the age of ninety.

CHAPTER 1

American Origins

A photograph of Upton Sinclair as a child of eight appears in his 1962 autobiography. More than anything else, the picture conveys a striking and unchildlike sense of seriousness. The boy's lips, with the upper one larger than the lower, are pressed firmly together but not pursed, making the line of the mouth horizontal without a trace of either a smile or a frown. The jaw is firm and the eyes penetrating. The position of the head is precocious and posed. The seriousness of the child's face suggests a sternness in his short life, an awareness of lessons already learned, an almost aristocratic sense of self, and, perhaps, a felt potential as a future minister, writer, or statesman. The same expression appears in all photographs of Sinclair.

The childhood behind the expression was painful, complex, and often contradictory. Its end result was a literary rebel who eventually became a Socialist, a muckraker, and a writer of international influence and reputation for over six decades. The roots of his remarkable career go back to a family life of middle-class values and upper-class connections combined with poverty and insecurity, Southern traditions combined with Northern urban experience, sexual ignorance combined with adolescent desire and religious moralism, and genteel literary influences combined with hack writing and visionary literary expectations. An understanding of his later attitudes and achievements must begin with the complicated story of his early years.

I Baltimore

Upton Beall Sinclair, Jr. was born in Baltimore on September 20, 1878, and lived there with his parents until he was eight or nine years old. According to his autobiographical writings,[1] his Baltimore childhood exerted an almost abnormal shaping power on his personality. The main source of this power was his divided and anxiety-ridden home. Its immediate result was an inward and reclusive bent that continued into later childhood and adolescence.

One source of anxiety in his home was the pressure of tradition. With the important exception of his father, Sinclair's paternal ancestors were well-known for their achievements as naval officers and their status as Virginia aristocrats. His great grandfather, for example, was a veteran of the Revolutionary War, a hero of the War of 1812, and one of the founders of the Naval Academy at Annapolis. By 1878 the Sinclair name had been admired and respected in Norfolk, Virginia, and in Maryland for over a hundred years. Yet, after the Civil War, during which the Sinclairs sided with the Confederacy, the family was stripped of property and position. What remained was pride and aristocratic bearing—of little practical value in post-War American life. Being among the displaced gentry of the South was especially tragic for Upton Beall Sinclair, Sr. Born shortly before the war, he grew up to find himself socially superfluous and occupationally disadvantaged. Handsome and sociable, he became a salesman, but he was not disposed to a commercial style of life, seldom made enough money, and soon became an alcoholic.

Upton Senior's life was an archetype of the post-War Southern temperament. He always gave the impression of being a "professional Southerner," full of "expansive phrases, of noble ideas derived from a vanished past, and wholly out of relation to a despised present."[2] For a while he was a wholesale whiskey distributor in Baltimore, and then he took a position in New York City as a seller of hats to haberdasheries. He never escaped his need to drink. In the presence of his only son he often tried to fight the demon, vowing to drink only beer or trying an expensive "cure" for alcoholism. These efforts never succeeded, and he died of delerium tremens in a New York hospital in 1907.

Upton Sinclair's mother, born Priscilla Harden, had been nutured on middle-class values and affluence, her father being not only secretary-treasurer of the Western Maryland Railroad but also a deacon of the Methodist Church. Prior to her own marriage one of her sisters had married the scion of an old Virginia family who soon became the president of a large trust company. When Priscilla Harden married, she may have been influenced by the Sinclair name as well as by her new husband's personality. Whatever the case, the union was eventually a disappointment to her. She had not bargained for financial insecurity and alcoholism. Consequently, she preached to her son a fear of all stimulants, including even coffee and tea, and condemned self-indulgence in general.[3]

Sinclair's early life at home, then, was one of division. He chased bedbugs in cheap rooming houses—often the only residence his father's salary allowed—and, at about the same time, enjoyed holidays with lavish quantities of food at his grandfather Harden's house. Furthermore, as an only child he was drawn into an unusually close relationship with his mother. His father's drinking, he later said, "caused me to follow my mother in everything."[4] He lacked early contact with other children, with male companions of any age, and with any form of behavior—besides his father's—that might have offended his mother. He did not even attend school until he was ten. Following his mother as he did, Sinclair grew up rejecting his father as a model of masculine behavior, feeling neither jealousy nor respect.[5]

Priscilla Sinclair valued books, both the English classics and popular novels, and provided an atmosphere of literacy for her son by reading stories to him and supplying him with children's books. By the time he was five, he could do much of his own reading, progressing quite early to the stories of Horatio Alger, *Pilgrim's Progress, Gulliver's Travels,* and the Bible. Reading had a special appeal for him, for it was a means of escaping his environment. Furthermore, he was drawn to the values and ideals in what he read. Unwilling to emulate his father, he was prepared for maturity largely by models of behavior in the printed word and by ideals that tended to coincide with those of his mother. This aspect of his nurture was, above all, genteel.

Sinclair's exposure to religion paralleled his early absorption of ideals through reading. At the home of his Methodist grandfather he read Bible stories and an assortment of Methodist literature, carefully studying, he later said, "all the pictures of the conflicts with the evil one."[6] In his own home he followed the Episcopalianism that his mother had taken up after her marriage. Priscilla Sinclair had little interest in fine distinctions of theology or denomination, but she conscientiously took her son to Sunday school and church, thereby providing him with a religious environment that became increasingly important to his sense of personal identity as he grew into adolescence.

Reared by his mother in the absence of other children and within a genteel culture, Sinclair was sheltered from sexual knowledge. His mother taught him the virtues of modesty and always implied that sex was "something dreadful" that one should scrupulously avoid mentioning. When Sinclair was later bewildered by the changes puberty brought about in his body, his mother "stood helplessly by, like the hen which hatches ducklings and sees them go into the water."[7] Understandably, sexuality later became a persistent subject in much of Sinclair's writing.

The facts of Sinclair's early years suggest that he was a typical "inner-directed" child of the nineteenth century. In his seminal work on American society, *The Lonely Crowd,* David Riesman identifies inner-directed child rearing as a process in which society encourages the child "to gird himself for the battle of life in the small circle of light cast by his reading lamp or candle."[8] This process was surely at work in Sinclair's development, as it was in the formative years of many nineteenth century Americans whose homes were essentially middle-class in spirit if not in substance, and it led to a rigid understanding of morality and a strong desire for achievement.

II *New York*

When Sinclair was eight or nine years old his family moved to New York City. For the following decade and a half, he spent at least nine months each year in the big city. Life there exerted a definite influence on his personality and on the direction of his career as a writer. The city pushed him into his first meaningful contact with the world outside his home, provided him with a public education, and eventually made it possible for him to earn a living of sorts with his pen.

In New York the small family established a pattern of living that was not much different from that in Baltimore. In the summers Sinclair and his mother usually left the city for more pleasant surroundings. During the rest of the year the three members of the family lived together in the city where they moved from cheap hotel to ramshackle boarding house to East Side flat, heeding the "cheaper to move than to pay rent" motto they had established in Baltimore. On several occasions they lived in a unique family hotel with other Southerners who had followed one American dream or another to New York. This place, the Weisinger House on West Nineteenth Street, where "half the broken-down aristocracy of the Old South" lived in an "oasis of gentility," made a lasting impression on Sinclair by magnifying his father's style of life and encouraging him to eventually reject his own past and search for alternate, even utopian, goals. [9]

The atmosphere of New York outside of the Weisinger house was less poisonous but still threatening to young Sinclair's idea of what was right and good. On one hand he made a real and often exciting contact with the non-Southern world and with other children, later claiming that in his New York childhood he "was one of nature's miracles, such as she produces by the millions in tenement streets— romping, shouting, and triumphant, entirely unaware that their lot is a miserable one." [10] On the other hand a suggestion of urban evil developed amid his sense of excitement. He saw firsthand the degeneracy in the Weisinger House; he heard the orations of reformers who spoke of vice and corruption throughout the city; he became too familiar with the saloons that he often had to enter to find his father; and, finally, he learned what prostitution was and how it was connected politically and economically with saloons and city officials. It is no surprise that the city later became the object of reform in Upton Sinclair's consciousness.

The city was also the setting of his formal education. His parents kept him out of school until shortly before his eleventh birthday in 1889, but in the following two years he made astonishing progress and completed all eight elementary grades. Then, when he turned fourteen in 1892, he entered the City College of New York.

In 1892 the "college" education Sinclair found at C.C.N.Y. was a five year course of study, the equivalent of a high school education and the first two years of college. It was designed for boys who could not afford preparatory school and college elsewhere, and as such it drew students largely from New York's growing Jewish population, from immigrants or the sons of immigrants. Upton Sinclair, with his Southern roots and his Methodist-Episcopalian sensibility, was undoubtedly out of place. Yet he successfully completed the school's "classical" curriculum of courses in the arts and sciences in order to prepare himself for a career as a lawyer. Later he changed his mind about the law, but throughout his years at C.C.N.Y. he apparently felt that the responsibilities of an attorney were compatible with his ideals.

At C.C.N.Y. Sinclair was a bookish student whose attitude towards school was sometimes tinged with skepticism. His Southern speech and dress, his refusal to violate genteel standards of conduct, and the shame he felt as a result of his father's continued drinking prevented him from making close friends at school. Study was congenial to him, though, and he did well in his classes—better at first than during his last two years. At times he showed promise in mathematics, but he was more interested in history, where his reading of pro-union works on the Civil War (including *Uncle Tom's Cabin*) gradually caused him to re-examine the Southern cause that his father respected with nostalgia and admiration. In literature classes, his experiences were often unpleasant, due to the Roman Catholic bias of some teachers who had gained their positions through the political pressure of Democratic (and therefore Irish Catholic) Tammany Hall. Such teachers, Sinclair later felt, tried to present "Catholic sentimentality disguised as poetry" to students who were mostly Jewish[11] and were probably the source of anti-Catholicism in several of his later books (especially *The Profits of Religion, The Goslings,* and *Our Lady*).

While Sinclair was at C.C.N.Y. he began his long career as a writer. His initial motivation was the near-poverty that he and his family continually faced. Since early childhood he had enjoyed the written word, and he assumed that writers were well paid for their efforts. When he was fifteen he began to submit puzzles and jokes to children's magazines, newspapers, and publishers of joke books. This was, of course, an odd beginning for an American radical writer; but at the time Sinclair must have been mainly aware that jokes and word games were often worth a dollar apiece, and that he had the capacity to produce them. "While other youths were thinking about 'dates,' " he said later, "I was pondering the jokableness of Scotchmen, Irishmen, Negroes, and Jews."[12] Many of the jokes he wrote do not seem very humorous today; yet at the age of sixteen he had discovered enough "jokableness" to pay the rent on a private room in New York—apparently in order to escape his father's presence—while his mother visited in Baltimore.

His writing efforts expanded to include fiction in 1895 when he sent a story off to a popular boys' magazine. The story—about the stealing of a pet bird by a Negro boy—was accepted by *Argosy,* and Sinclair received the considerable sum of twenty-five dollars for his achievement. Stimulated by this kind of compensation, he began to devote all of his effort to turning out stories for juvenile periodicals and for the "Children's Page" of New York newspapers. Thereafter—he was sixteen at the time—Sinclair earned his living exclusively with his pen. In later years he was fond of boasting that he never earned a cent in any other fashion.

Although Sinclair's early writing was above all else a possible way out of the economic and social situation of his family, there were other satisfactions involved. Writing was obviously a way of rebelling against the irrelevance of many college classes, against the occupational hopes his parents held for him, and, especially, against the emotional burden he bore as the son of an alcoholic. In a story published in 1896 in a C.C.N.Y. literary magazine, for instance, he subsumed the antipathy he felt for his father by telling of a lazy Virginia black who gets drunk and then gets thrown into jail as a lunatic. [13]

Sinclair continued to write juvenile stories off and on for six or seven years after 1895 and the careless style of this hack work showed up later in much of his mature writing. However, after 1896, even as he continued to be a juvenile hack, his literary interests became increasingly serious, first in reading, then in writing. Behind this change lay the religious experiences of his New York adolescence.

III *Reverend Moir*

Sinclair's life and works clearly indicate that he was a religious seeker throughout his early life and, later, an evangelist for the gospel of social reform. This is not to say that his gestures as an American radical were merely attempts to satisfy personal religious needs. It is obvious, however, that an important source of Sinclair's radical sensibility was his early enthusiasm for traditional Protestant moralism—an enthusiasm which remained with him when aesthetic or social doctrines later displaced his belief in religious dogma. This formative religiosity developed strongly between the ages of thirteen and eighteen as he attended college, exploited his initial interest in writing, and lived through the emotional weather of puberty.

Sinclair's chief source of religious enthusiasm during adolescence was a young Episcopal minister, William Wilmerding Moir. Later, around eighteen, Sinclair grew skeptical of orthodox theology, but he was never free afterwards of a strong religious and moralistic impulse set in motion largely by Reverend Moir. "I have never forgotten this loving soul and what he meant to me at the critical time in my life," Sinclair later wrote. [14] The son of a wealthy merchant, Moir had given up wealth and fashion for the clergy. As Sinclair did later, he took seriously the social precepts of Christianity and honestly felt that a rich man had no place in heaven.

There was, however, another side to Moir. He accepted with great seriousness the attitude of St. Paul towards extramartial sex and told Sinclair and other young protégés that he had personally defeated an extraordinary, sinful, and debilitating sexual urge. In Sinclair's autobiographical novel *Love's Pilgrimage* Moir appears as a young divinity student named Warner whose life "had been one torment because of the cravings of lust" and who therefore disapproved of all forms of sensual pleasure—the theater, dancing, "impassioned poetry," and "all non-religious music"—because it somehow appealed to his sexual hunger.[15]

Moir apparently felt that repression of sexual desire would enhance one's mental and spiritual powers—and he passed this doctrine on to a number of adolescent boys, Sinclair included, who met once a month to hear him explain the dangers of extramarital sex and preach the virtues of chastity. For the boys who met with him, of course, Moir was far more than a dispenser of sexual fears. Like Horatio Alger, whom he may have admired, his concern for the boys was obviously fatherly, and he was often instrumental in finding jobs for them in the city. Sinclair recognized and eagerly responded to such concern. In doing so he accepted a religious moralism that demanded both social conscience and extreme self-control. In *Love's Pilgrimage* he indicates that as an adolescent he was tormented by "storms of craving" for women but was always restrained by the lessons he learned from Moir and by a "dream of a noble and beautiful love" in which he believed.[16] Partly in hyperbole, his novel says that outwardly he was like other youths, but within himself he felt "a hidden thing which brooded and questioned" and "a fear that self-indulgence might lay its grisly paws upon him."[17]

Sinclair experienced a crisis of religious faith around the age of eighteen. What happened then, for reasons that are not perfectly clear in any of his autobiographical accounts, was a failure of his belief in the trans-mundane God of traditional Christianity. The ostensible reason for this change was intellectual, and in his autobiography Sinclair says that when Moir naively gave him several volumes of Episcopal apologetics to read, their logical inconsistencies drove him to agnosticism. Whatever the underlying causes, it is perfectly clear that in late adolescence Sinclair was no longer able to accept orthodox Christian doctrine, especially the idea of an afterlife dependent on faith. Yet he retained the capacity for enthusiasm, idealism, and self-control that had characterized his attachment to the church and to the teachings of Reverend Moir.

In short, Sinclair experienced an "identity crisis" that involved, as did other crises of identity among sensitive youth in nineteenth-century America,[18] an extensive emotional investment in traditional supernatural Christianity. During this typical but intense struggle for identity, which continued until Sinclair's late twenties, he followed a path from orthodox Protestantism under Reverend Moir to a worship of literature and a notion of himself as a poetic "genius" and, finally, to a faith in pre-World War I American Socialism. It was, for Sinclair, an arduous journey, but it was not untypical for his times. Neither was it especially direct, nor was the destination always completely satisfactory.

IV *The Genius and the Hack*

No period in Sinclair's early life was more important to the development of his writing interests than the period from 1896 to 1900. During these four late adolescent years he underwent a series of emotional, religious, intellectual, and literary experiences that culminated in a new certainty of himself as a poetic "genius" and in a decision to leave home and school in order to write what he thought would be the "great American novel."

Much of what happened to Sinclair during these years was undoubtedly caused by a rapidly deteriorating situation in his home. His father apparently began to show advanced symptoms of alcoholism, often disappearing for a week or two at a time and even requiring hospitalization on occasions.[19] Also, since his father unwillingly forced his mother to grow more dependent on her son for emotional support and income, Sinclair had further reason to dislike his life at home and to dream of independence.

At the same time he was experiencing religious doubts concerning the divinity of Jesus and the possibility of spiritual salvation, and was questioning the relationship between Sunday school lessons and the problems of life outside the church.[20] It seems obvious that he may indeed have had serious difficulty in looking beyond his unhappy home to the promise of orthodox Christianity.

Although the young Sinclair may have found it theologically or intellectually impossible to maintain his belief in supernatural Christianity, he was not long in attaching his religious intensity to a new and, for him, equally powerful faith. This new faith was a form of literary Romanticism. Between his eighteenth and twenty-second birthdays he began to believe in a special aesthetic and intellectual dispensation granted to true artists and leaders. For him—and for others of his time—this quality was "genius."

Sinclair experienced what he took to be evidence of his own possession of genius in 1896. Dissatisfied with college and perhaps with his hack writing, he began to devote more attention to serious literature. In his senior English class at C.C.N.Y. he was strongly drawn to Shakespeare and Shelley, especially the latter. His literary "idols," in fact, soon became an odd triumvirate of Jesus, Hamlet, and Shelley—two real persons and one literary character. The quality of genius in him, however, seemed to be confirmed primarily by profound emotional experiences, the first of which occurred during the Christmas holidays of 1896. He was then in Baltimore visiting at an uncle's home where he found volumes of Milton and Shakespeare that he read "with love and rapture" for fourteen hours a day. While walking in a nearby park one night towards the end of this reading period, he experienced the following rapturous sensations:

Suddenly this thing came to me, startling and wonderful beyond any power of words to tell; the opening of gates in the soul, the pouring in of music, of light, of joy that was unlike anything else, and therefore not to be conveyed in metaphors. I stood riveted to one spot, and a trembling seized me, a dizziness, a happiness so intense that the distinction between pleasure and pain was lost.

If I had been a religious person at this time, no doubt I would have had visions of saints and holy martyrs, and perhaps have developed stigmata on hands and feet. But I had no sort of superstition, so the vision took a literary form. There was a campfire by a mountain road, to which came travelers who hailed one another and made high revelry there without alcohol. Yes, even Falstaff and Prince Hal were purified and refined, according to my teetotal sentiments! There came the melancholy Prince of Denmark, and Don Quixote—I must have been reading him at this time. Also Shelley—real persons mixed with imaginary ones, but all equal in this realm of fantasy. . . . I was laughing, singing with the delight of their company; in short, a perfect picture of a madman, talking to myself, making incoherent exclamations. Yet I knew what I was doing, I knew what was happening, I knew that this was literature, and that if I could remember the tenth part of it and set it down on paper it would be read.[21]

This kind of experience revisited Sinclair on occasion for the rest of his life. He called it "ecstasy" and felt that it confirmed his potential as a serious writer. "Even now," he wrote when he was seventy-eight, "in my old age I go out in my garden and walk, and a chapter of a new book I am writing unrolls itself in my mind. I cannot tell how it happens . . . it is always a marvellous thing to me, all the problems of construction are answered."[22]

Sinclair's "ecstasy" may seem ludicrous, but it cannot be passed over lightly. Its early manifestations may have been a means of escape from a painful environment by associating, in imagination, with princes and heroes. At the very least, its presence indicates an indelible strain of Romanticism in the career of a twentieth century Socialist and muckraker.

After his first intimation of genius in late 1896 Sinclair began to read Romantic literature with ever increasing interest. Near the end of his fifth year at C.C.N.Y., in the spring of 1897, he took a month's leave of absence from college to immerse himself in Shelley, Carlyle, and Emerson. He was growing bored by his college classes, and attracted almost religiously to the notion of the artist as neo-spiritual creator or, in Shelley's words, as one of the "unacknowledged legislators of the world."

That fall he entered Columbia University to spend a year studying literature and philosophy before going on to law school. His one year stretched into three, and he never made it to law school. Instead, he decided to make a career out of his serious desire for expression. He spent much of his time outside class turning out boys' adventure stories. In classrooms he sampled many courses and completed those related to his own changing interests. He was intrigued by courses like one on "Practical Ethics," which dealt with political reform, and one on Renaissance history under James Harvey Robinson, which stressed the role of iconoclasts like Erasmus and Luther in the making of modern civilization. He was most interested, however, in learning about music from Edward MacDowell, and in studying literature under George Edward Woodberry. Both teachers strongly influenced his developing ideas concerning creative expression. A Romantic and a worshipper of Beethoven, MacDowell believed in "the subordination of techniques to the vital spirit of art," and insisted that his students should "go out into the world and make beautiful and inspiring and human art."[23] Woodberry stressed the moral force of genius in Western literature and the need for poets to oppose materialism on aesthetic grounds; Romantic poets like Emerson and Shelley, Woodberry felt, had pointed the way towards a new and more meaningful form of Christianity.[24]

While Sinclair cultivated his idealism at Columbia under the tutelage of MacDowell and Woodberry, however, he found it financially necessary to keep writing stories for boys. In fact, during his final year at C.C.N.Y. he had accepted an offer from the publishing house of Street and Smith to write two adventure series for the firm's juvenile magazines. For almost two years thereafter he wrote the weekly adventures of a fictional West Point cadet and an Annapolis counterpart. Altogether, while attending C.C.N.Y. and Columbia, he composed about ninety stories for *Army and Navy Weekly* and other Street and Smith publications. He later claimed to have kept two stenographers continually busy as he dictated stories every afternoon and worked over the previous day's copy in the evenings.[25]

Fantasy and wish fulfillment define these stories. Sinclair's two protagonists are his age, both have lost their fathers, and both must support crippled or chronically ill mothers. But they are gregarious and extroverted youths of action and their luck and pluck wins them fortune and therefore freedom from the burden of supporting their mothers. Then, as military cadets, they trounce bullies, stealthily creep through strange and distant jungles, and patriotically finish off America's enemies in Cuba and the Philippines. Oddly, none of the episodes exhibit nascent radicalism; one even ridicules Populism (promoted by "hayseeds") while extolling the virtues of the idly rich friends of a West Point youth.[26]

This kind of apprenticeship schooled Sinclair in glib diction and coincidental plot, and it paid him forty dollars a week. Understandably, he longed for freedom to explore and express more serious material. One of the results of this longing, in 1899, was a lengthy article, "Unity and Infinity in Art," in which he explained his ideas about art and its creation. Published in *The Metaphysical Magazine*, a New York theosophist journal catering to vaguely occult expressions, Sinclair's first serious publication indicates the shape of his literary thought prior to his discovery of Socialism. Art, including literature, his essay says, is an essentially religious preoccupation which, when guided by genius, presages a future heaven on earth.

Sinclair indicated that true artists are "pioneers of humanity" who prophetically "catch the first rays of the dawn" and "sing of its coming."[27] Such visionary artists perceive "Truth Absolute," live virtue as well as sing it, yet have an understanding as well of the concrete world. Although there is a mystical strain in Sinclair's assumption that in the future seen by true artists "the veil that hides the deity shall by rent away and all things shall be One," his article is mostly a buoyant rendition of Shelley's (and George Edward Woodberry's) idea that poets are "the mirrors of the gigantic shadows which futurity casts upon the present."[28]

Written several years before Sinclair became a Socialist, "Unity and Infinity in Art" illuminates the author's early preparation for his later literary and political roles. His stated belief in the coming "dawn" of humanity was later transformed into the idea of a Socialist millennium. More importantly, in 1899 the young Sinclair affirmed a utopian function for art: he indicated that the artist was visionary in his powers and possibly revolutionary but also a master of concrete fact. Such he later tried to be as a propagandist and a muckraker.

These formulations and foreshadowings in 1899 came amid emotional, intellectual, and religious problems of late adolescence. The problems became increasingly insistent during Sinclair's second and third years at Columbia. He was bound by emotion and responsibility to a depressing home life, but he yearned for the freedom to write as he felt he could if not restrained by the demands of hack fiction. His autobiography indicates that at this time the outside world, especially classes at Columbia, had become for him largely dull and empty. Also, he no longer had any desire to become a lawyer, and the idea of a business career was an anathema to him. By early 1900, at the age of twenty-one, Upton Sinclair wanted only to "create literature" on his own terms and in his own way. He had "in a spiritual sense, become pregnant," he later claimed, and felt compelled to give life to a serious novel that was filling his consciousness.[29] Hopefully, he would join the ranks of artists and poets, and thereby rise above the oppressive confines of his daily life.

CHAPTER 2

From Genius to Socialist

SINCLAIR chose a propitious moment to launch his career as a serious writer. The year of 1900 marked the end of the remarkable American literary decade of the 1890's. Stephen Crane died in June. In November Dreiser's *Sister Carrie* appeared, only to be suppressed by its publisher. The previous year Kate Chopin's *The Awakening* had been criticized into oblivion. Within two years Frank Norris would die of peritonitis, his epic trilogy of wheat unfinished. With the possible exception of Jack London, American letters were apparently doomed to a resurgence of idealism and gentility. Sinclair did not start out to buck the tide. His literary mentors came from on high: Shelley, Emerson, Shakespeare, Jesus. His interest in the concrete was eroded by his yearning to perceive infinity. Conceivably, Sinclair could have written from his own observations, dealing with urban life as he had seen it, oppression as he had felt it, division and despair as unavoidable aspects of existence, felt sexuality as a contrast to genteel moralism. Schooled in writing for mass circulation, he might have developed a style free of the stale ornamentation and clichés of elite expression. That he did not do these things indicates that he was trapped—temporarily, at least—within the conventions of his culture. He had little interest in the critical and realistic perceptions of writers like Twain, Howells, and Crane.

His identification of his literary concerns in 1900 as "spiritual" may seem paradoxical in view of the muckraker he later became. Yet there is a clear line of development between his early idealism and his later radical expressions. Between 1900 and 1904, through a transformation of genteel expectations into radical political ideas, he became the kind of writer who could write *The Jungle*. These were apprentice years. Ideologically, Sinclair was influenced by iconoclastic Nietzschean egotism and the contrasting doctrines of Socialism. These years were also marked by unsuccessful striving, poverty, strained personal and sexual relations, bitterness, and—eventually—a kind of identification with American history that was necessary for his later devotion to social justice.

I Springtime and Harvest

In May of 1900 Sinclair gave up his studies at Columbia and moved to a small cabin in the woods of Quebec in order to write what he imagined would be the "great American novel."[1] Enjoying occasional ecstasies, he worked alone for a couple of months until his mother visited the area and introduced him to Meta Fuller, a daughter of a friend. Meta, who had known Sinclair in childhood, was impressed by his intentions to tell a story of "high and noble love," and Sinclair was drawn to Meta's "extraordinary sense of purity."[2] Consequently, the couple fell in love. According to the autobiographical *Love's Pilgrimage*, they spent much time discussing his novel, his genius, and his idea of himself as "an art work" sacrificed "for what other people ought to be."[3] Apparently feeling that marriage and sex might hinder Sinclair's creativity, they decided to maintain a strictly platonic relationship.

Springtime and Harvest, the novel that Sinclair wrote that summer of 1900, did not quite achieve the rank of "great American novel." Highly influenced by his love affair, it is flawed by excess sentimentality and by lengthy purple passages of didactic philosophizing. Yet it is an important document in Sinclair's career and thematically his germinal work of fiction.

Sinclair later claimed to have based his story on the life of a beautiful woman he knew who married a crippled man for his money but instead "came to understand his really fine mind."[4] Something like this happens in *Springtime and Harvest* when a young woman, Helen, refuses to marry an insensitive railroad president and chooses instead a sickly, middle-aged poet named David Howard. After her marriage to the poet, Helen learns that he had once been wealthy and promiscuous before his conversion to beauty, love, and poetry; he is, in fact, the father of a younger man of poetic inclination who has always been in love with Helen. Unfortunately, Helen's happy marriage ends when David Howard sickens and dies. But before he passes away he pleads with Helen to retain his vision of purpose in life—a vision unsullied by any belief in an afterlife—and not to grieve when he is gone. After his death Helen nobly transcends her sorrow. At the end of the novel she preaches Howard's (he is always Mr. Howard to her) philosophy of life to his illegitimate son Arthur.

Sinclair's consideration of such a story as fit material for *the* great

American work of fiction suggests that he believed that America's most important potential was its possibility of avoiding materialism. (It is instructive to note that in the same year Dreiser wrote his version of the great American novel in *Sister Carrie*—also a first attempt at long fiction—and suggested that Americans were unable to be anything but materialistic.) This aesthetic anti-materialism and a rejection of Christian supernaturalism are the two most important ideological aspects of *Springtime and Harvest*. At the beginning of his career as a novelist, Sinclair expressed a demanding and expectant philosophy of life, a kind of naturalized Calvinism, freed of thoughts of an afterlife, in which labor, love, and achievement are held sacred. Strangely, these early aspects of Sinclair's idealism would lead him first into an admiration of Nietzsche's "Overman" and then later into the American Socialist movement.

It is also important to notice that in Sinclair's first novel his protagonist perceives social injustice in the world and criticizes men of wealth who "are eating the bread of honest men while millions are toiling and starving in order that they may have ease and luxury."[5] In spite of this neo-Marxist understanding of economics, Howard does not think that one can do much about social injustice besides "keep his own life earnest and true," which means stripped to the material essentials. Although *Springtime and Harvest* contains an implicit criticism of American materialism, the purpose of the novel was not reform. Set in an idealized countryside and somehow free from any financial problems, the idyll of Helen and David Howard clearly expresses a wish for freedom from the corrupting influence of urban America.

II *Marriage and Survival*

In late summer of 1900 Sinclair finished his manuscript of *Springtime and Harvest* and returned to New York City after a short visit with his old friend Reverend Moir at Lake Placid. Back in the city he faced two difficult problems: how to get his work before the American public, and what to do about Meta Fuller. He first attempted to solve the latter problem by investing large amounts of time in studying and talking with Meta. Although he did not want to marry at the time—because he felt that his chief responsibility was to his writing and both he and Meta felt that their love affair was above the level of sexual needs—he bowed to the pressure of his and her parents, who, according to Sinclair's account in his autobiography, found the brother and sister relationship difficult to understand. He and Meta were married on October 18 in the study of Minot J. Savage, a Unitarian minister and writer (especially of psychic phenomena) whom Sinclair admired.

The marriage was unfortunate in many respects. Not only did it interfere with Sinclair's freedom to write by demanding some measure of financial security, but it also joined together two persons with differing emotional needs. According to Sinclair's autobiographical works, the source of difficulty in the marriage was largely sexual. Although Meta and Sinclair at first decided that they could do without sex, a family doctor soon convinced Sinclair that abstention was potentially dangerous to Meta's health. Once the couple began to engage in sexual relations, Sinclair suffered greatly from feelings of shame and entrapment while Meta found sexual intercourse to be "an utter blending of two selves, the losing of one's personality in another."[6] This difference in sexual response was to plague Sinclair throughout his marriage with Meta, which ended in divorce in 1912. For more than a decade Sinclair was pulled in one direction by his idealism and in an opposite direction by his responsibilities first as husband and then as husband and father.

Sinclair's marriage was also overshadowed from its beginning by his failure in the literary marketplace. In the fall and early winter of 1900, a series of publishers rejected *Springtime and Harvest*. These rejections greatly dismayed Sinclair; he felt that his book was far better than the majority of novels then being offered for public consumption. He was wrong, of course, if he thought that his story was highly interesting, but he was certain enough of his achievement to emulate Stephen Crane and publish the novel himself. Consequently, after a loan from a relative, the "Sinclair Press" issued *Springtime and Harvest* in January 1901. But even after sending out nearly a hundred review copies, the enterprising young author sold only enough books, mostly to personal acquaintances, to repay the loan. A contributing reason for the failure of the book may have been a brash introduction which Sinclair composed, describing the story as a "fearful work" which had required from its author not only courage to write but also "a conviction to sell it . . . to get down into the arena and see the fight through himself, to carve out with his own hands a place in the world for his ideal."[7]

Shortly afterwards, in the spring of 1901, Sinclair learned that Meta vas pregnant—a contingency that he had hoped to avoid and which, when combined with the failure of his novel and the demands of relatives that he find a regular job, brought about an emotional crisis in his life. He later said that he and Meta considered abortion before rejecting the idea on ethical grounds. Obviously, he felt trapped, as he later said, "in a cage, the bars being made not of steel, but of human beings."[8]

The bars grew less rigid when the publishing company of Funk and Wagnalls expressed an interest in reissuing *Springtime and Harvest* under their imprint and with a new title. These developments encouraged Sinclair to consider writing another novel, one based on his insight into the evils of commercialism and a developing skepticism about the ability of genius to shape reality. To provide the space and atmosphere required by his imagination, he and Meta moved out of the city during the summer of 1901. They set up housekeeping in a tent on one of the Thousands Islands, where he worked on *Prince Hagen*, a novel which he published two years later.

III   Prince Hagen

For *Prince Hagen* Sinclair drew upon a reserve of fantasy which was partly the product of his admiration for Wagner and German Romanticism and partly the product of his hack work days. The novel tells the story of a gold seeking Nibelung who amazingly turns up in America and successively becomes a Tammany organizer, a Republican orator, and finally an unscrupulous Wall Street financier. Fortunately, Hagen dies while exercising two new Arabian horses on the day he is scheduled to marry into a prominent New York City family. The attack on American materialism and political corruption is heavy-handed throughout the book.

Not only does this second novel indicate Sinclair's willingness to work with fantasy rather than reality, but it also suggests an inchoate pessimism shortly before his discovery of the Socialist movement. This pessimism is most obvious in the ironic inability of the narrator, a young poet intent upon impressing Prince Hagen with the virtues of a Christian sensibility, to bring off any kind of reform. The narrator, identified as an "idealist," is certain that things must be changed in America, "this huge, overgrown civilization of ours, this vast, machine-built jungle, where bigness is so much taken for granted, and greediness for power." Furthermore, he is certain that American materialism and corrupton "must be the fault of the artists, who are its soul; there being among them no man with any thought of strenuous living or of the need of truth, nor soul to scourge the selfishness and fire the hearts of the coming men with generous emotion and resolve."[9] Yet, in the end America is too big for this one artist. Hagan, greedy troll that he really is, is a perfect American success story until his unlucky accident.

As his creator was often to do in the following decades, the narrator-poet of *Prince Hagen* preaches moral uplift and exhorts America to honor ideals rather than possessions. His rhetoric is unsuccessful, though, and the real implication of the novel is that American greediness cannot be corrected short of revolution. Sinclair does not state this conclusion in any obvious way in the story but, contradicting the hopefulness of *Springtime and Harvest,* his underlying logic casts much doubt on the effectiveness of Romantic idealism as a force for social change. *Prince Hagen,* then, is one of the few Sinclair novels which cast a shadow of irony on Sinclair's own intentions.

IV   The Overman

In the fall of 1901 Sinclair and his wife moved back to the city for a second consecutive winter of frustrated publishing hopes, personal hardships, and family complaints. This time the birth of a child made their winter stay even more difficult. Yet Sinclair had no intentions of giving up his dreams of success—not even when he failed to find a publisher for *Prince Hagen* or when the reissued version of his first novel, now entitled *King Midas* (apparently to stress the fact that a poet like David Howard can turn experience into gold), was a commercial failure in spite of a large number of friendly reviews.

At the time he undoubtedly found the roles of husband and expectant father difficult to assume. He refused to find a steady, nonliterary job, and when he tried to fall back upon his hack work for income he found that his ability to write boys' adventure stories had been ruined by his attempts at serious fiction. He was able to earn money only by writing a few short articles and unsigned reviews for the *Independent* and the *Literary Review.* At times he even wrote letters begging public spirited persons to read his work and save him from starvation by lending him money.[10]

Nearly destitute after the birth of a son, David, in midwinter, Sinclair moved his wife and child into her family's apartment while he spend the rest of the winter in a cheap upper room in the same building, where he wrote intensively. His most significant composition in early 1902 was a short novel, published in 1907 as *The Overman,* expressing his ebullient discovery of Friedrich Nietzsche.

Sinclair read *Thus Spake Zarathustra* in late 1901 or early 1902, seven years before the first English translation of the book and six years before H. L. Mencken began to write praises of Nietzsche. Read in its original German, *Zarathustra* reaffirmed Sinclair's faith in his own genius. After *Prince Hagan*, which took note of social problems in spite of its fantasy and pessimism, Sinclair turned about face and wrote a scenario of the apocalyptic inner life which he had glimpsed in Nietzsche. Asserting that the artist is capable of solipsistically experiencing "rapture and unutterable holiness," *The Overman* was Sinclair's most extreme statement of the Romantic possibilities of self.

The title of the short novel is a reference to Nietzsche's *uber-mensch* (usually translated as "superman"). Its plot concerns a promising musician named Daniel who is shipwrecked on an uninhabited Pacific island for twenty years until he is discovered by his brother, a scientist. Daniel tells his objective minded brother that he first regretted his isolation and inability to publish his musical compositions. But he soon learned, he says, to create music and to appreciate it without writing it down or hearing it played. This proved to him that "each individual soul is a microcosm self-sufficient, and its own excuse for being." Furthermore, at times he has felt his inner feelings pass out of his control and through an "indescribable fear" and "a sudden rending away of barriers" become a mystical ecstasy in which he stands "transfixed with the glory of an endless vision of dawn." By now, after years of solitude, Daniel has even managed to achieve ecstasy through "an effort of will," and thereby enter a realm of consciousness where inspiration reigns but, because there are no thoughts of immortality, "the essence of life is sorrow." Daniel likens his feelings during ecstasy to "a soldier in the crisis of battle, panting, and blind with pain, dying amid the glory of his achievement."[11]

The Overman may legitimately be dismissed as the wild product of a momentary exuberance over Nietzsche, yet there is no evidence that Sinclair was not entirely serious in writing the story. He allowed the book to be published several times after *The Jungle* came out in 1906. *The Overman* remains, therefore, an intriguing document, and it suggests that Sinclair's ultimate vision of experience in 1902 was an odd combination of the aesthetic and the physical. The twenty-three year old writer felt—or wanted to feel—that perfect ecstasy could be achieved by the individual alone, with no help from either society or nature. Although the resulting mystical experience would include inspiration and beauty, it would be accompanied by physical sensations like those felt in battle—or possibly even like those felt during sexual intercourse. Wishfulness on Sinclair's part seems to lie behind this kind of vision—a wishfulness perhaps reflecting a lack of meaningful experience in his life at the time.

However, the inclusion of sorrow and mortality as ingredients of the ecstasy in *The Overman* also suggests a strong religiosity—or at the very least an intense seriousness—at work in Sinclair's imagination. It is hardly surprising that the type of Socialism that he later developed such great passions for was couched, for him at least, in a rhetoric with underlying religious implications.

V   Arthur Stirling

During the first three months of 1902, after writing *The Overman*, Sinclair grew more anxious about his fate as a writer. Unlike his Nietzschean hero he was not able to live completely within himself because he had the responsibility of supporting both a son and a wife. Instead of sharing his inspiration, his wife now lived a life of dull routine, post-maternity depression, and illness. A fear of capitulating to economic necessity in the form of an uninspirational job haunted Sinclair. As a compromise he approached a publisher (probably Funk and Wagnalls) with the idea of writing a "practical" novel about a "plain everyday young author" struggling to make himself known; he promised not to create a "rebel and a frenzied egotist" as he had done before.[12]

Apparently aware of Sinclair's dedication to fiction, an editor of the publishing firm agreed to the idea and promised to supply him with occasional review work while he wrote his practical novel. Sinclair then decided to return alone to the Thousand Islands where he had written *Prince Hagen* the year before, in order to write his new story. Alone in the woods he once again wrote about himself, this time in an even less disguised form than ever before, and thus ended with a tale of a rebel and a frenzied egotist. The title of his book, a long fictitious journal, was *The Journal of Arthur Stirling*. As he wrote it, in six weeks of intense composition, he was sustained by *Thus Spake Zarathustra*, which he had remembered to withdraw from the Columbia library before leaving New York City.[13]

The Journal of Arthur Stirling records a young artist's gradual awakening to the tragic nature of existence. Arthur Stirling, once a mere cable car conductor, feels a "demon in his soul" that drives him to compose a long blank verse drama entitled *The Captive*, which tells of a prisoner who commits suicide rather than submit to torture. He feels that his poem, even though its style is subservient to its subject matter, is clearly in the tradition of *Prometheus Bound,* *Prometheus Unbound,* and *Samson Agonistes.* In his journal, which he keeps as he writes *The Captive* (but which does not include more than occasional excerpts from the poem), he muses on the nature of the poet. The poet, he says, referring both to himself and obviously to Sinclair, finds truth in his own being and at last learns that his "salvation" is "to rest never, and to toil always, and to dwell in this Presence of his God." The "Presence" is of course within the self. Stirling identifies this compulsive striving as "the Religion of Evolution"—apparently, moral evolution depends on such efforts by men of genius. Jesus, he claims, extolled such a sensibility, and Nietzsche is now its spokesman. For Arthur Stirling himself, however, such a strenuous philosophy of self is eventually frustrated by the refusal of any publisher to accept *The Captive.* Unable to toil always without public recognition and compensation, Arthur Stirling commits suicide by drowning—after making arrangments with a friend for the survival of his journal.[14]

Sinclair had this fictitious journal published a year later as the actual literary remains of a suicidal poet—a hoax, unique in American literature, which worked for a few weeks until some reviewers noticed the stylistic similarity between it and *King Midas.* The set of ideas that Sinclair apparently hoped to express in his work now seems contradictory. Sinclair tries through his persona to express a solipsistic philosophy which substitutes the self for God but vitiates the value of solipsism by having Stirling commit suicide at the end. What he really indicates is a genuine American hunger for public success. According to Kenneth S. Lynn's *The Dream of Success: A Study of the Modern American Imagination* (Boston, 1955), such a desire for success, combined with a paradoxical willingness to criticize material success in general, is particularly identifiable in important American novelists between 1890 and 1920, especially in Norris, London, and Dreiser. In the case of Arthur Stirling's "journal," it is important to realize that if Stirling had really been a follower of Nietzsche's individualism, which asserts the foolishness of trying to communicate with the "herd," he would not have been upset to the point of suicide when publishers turned down his work. Sinclair's book smacks of Goethe's *The Sorrows of Young Werther* more than it does of Nietzsche.

The Jornal of Arthur Stirling is of course of greater biographical than literary value. It suggests bitterness rather than art, and it offers few inducements to empathy. Yet, the novel unmistakably points up the tension that Sinclair felt early in his career between an individualistic, Romantic vision of ideality and a psychological and social need to be accepted, to have a recognized role, in the larger community. Throughout most of the time immediately previous to his acceptance of Socialism, Sinclair obviously tried to reject his social self in favor of his notion of genius.

By 1902 he had tested his inner certitudes—his idealism, his belief in the working of poetic genius—against his society and had found one, self or society, or perhaps both, lacking. *Arthur Stirling* was, in effect, an admission that he could not continue his resistance to society in the same manner that he had been following for three years. That Sinclair himself was actually considering suicide at the time is doubtful. Nevertheless, the suicide of Arthur Stirling was an admission, perhaps unconscious, that his own Romantic rebellion was nearing its end. In 1902 and 1903, Sinclair was faced with a choice between defeat, most likely in the form of accepting an established role in society, or the discovery of a new and more effective means of self-expression. Socialism finally indicated a way of using creative powers as a means of serving others and as a way of achieving a meaningful and recognized identity within a community of human beings. As Sinclair accepted the communitarian ethos of Socialism, his literary efforts moved away from the lure of solipsism to a greater awareness of social reality.

VI   *Socialism*

When Sinclair finished *The Journal of Arthur Stirling* early in the summer of 1902, he discovered that his original publisher was not pleased with his out of the ordinary manuscript. But his efforts were saved by D. Appleton and Company, which agreed to publish the book the following January. Before this date, Sinclair published an anonymous article entitled "Confessions of a Young Author" in the *Independent*. His "Confession" was an attempt to contrast the ease with which he had sold his hack work with the great difficulty he had in publishing and selling his serious literary efforts. He did not mention the soon to be published journal, but he concluded his article cryptically by saying "I still have the fight to win" and "you will hear of me . . . someday."[15] Such undirected personal bitterness and arrogance was soon focused, and somewhat mollified, by an awareness of Socialism.

His introduction to Socialism was fortuitous. It occurred when he visited the offices of the *Literary Digest* and met there another visitor, a "gentle-souled" young man named Leonard D. Abbot. Abbot, a Socialist, gave Sinclair a number of panphlets, led him next door to meet John Spargo, editor of the Socialist journal *The Comrade*, and later introduced him to other prominent Socialists, including Gaylord Wilshire, the millionaire publisher of *Wilshire's Magazine*, and George D. Herron, formerly a Congregationalist preacher and professor of theology. Although Sinclair later described his first awareness of Socialism as the ideological turning point of his life, "the falling down of prison walls about my mind,"[16] he was also certainly impressed that many of the members of the Socialist Party of America in 1902—Abbot, Wilshire, and Herron—were educated, idealistic and often wealthy. Previously, in his opinion of populism at least, he had considered radical politics "vulgar, noisy, and beneath my cultured contempt."[17]

It took Sinclair several years to grasp the proletarian and reformist aspects of Socialism. However, from the beginning, it appears that he understood the way in which many Socialists accepted Socialism as the culmination of Christianity. George D. Herron, a powerful spokesman for the Social Gospel since 1890, contributed most significantly to this awareness. From the chair of Applied Christianity at Iowa (later Grinnell) College, Herron had preached the message of sacrifice as the answer to social problems in America, and of Jesus as the model for modern man. Society had departed from the way of Christ, he said, by assuming that competition is order; competition is anarchy, he felt, and its product is "the unspeakably corrupt world of business."[18] Herron eventually advocated complete Socialism, which he identified at times with the force of God at work in society. His Socialism was thus decidedly chiliastic and evangelistic, as was his personality. To Sinclair he conveyed a sense "of gigantic issues, of age long destinies hanging in the balance, embracing hopes and powers struggling to be born"[19]—a sense that led Sinclair to admire and correspond with him for over twenty years.

Under Herron's influence Sinclair did not become a Marxian or "scientific" Socialist immediately. Undoubtedly he was first attracted to the explanation that Socialism provided for his failure to be recognized as a true artist—Americans were intellectually as well as economically corrupted by competition and business. He spent much time making new acquaintances within the Socialist elite, and during the winter of 1902–1903 he wrote a short novel, entitled *A Captain of Industry* when it was published in 1906, from a neo-Socialist perspective.

A *Captain of Industry* tells the story of a wealthy man, Robert Van Renssalaer, who reaps what he sows. Van Renssalaer leads a profligate life as a young man and sleeps with a poor girl whom his father will not allow him to marry. As an adult he becomes a cruel industrialist who crushes a strike at his "Hungryville Mills Company." Later he takes as his mistress a young woman who turns out to be his own illegitimate daughter. When he and his mistress-daughter discover this fact, precisely at the moment when he is becoming the world's richest man by manipulating the stock market, she commits suicide. He then sails off on his yacht into a storm which swamps the vessel and batters him against the rocks on the Atlantic coast. Afterwards, "unnumerable small creatures" feed on the face of the "swollen and purple" body.[20]

Like several novels that Sinclair would later write, A *Captain of Industry* is unsophisticated as fiction and weak as Socialist doctrine. Unlike *Prince Hagan,* which it resembles in plot, it lacks even a modicum of sympathy for the protagonist-villain. Furthermore, it suggests that the power of money and class to corrupt can only be opposed by the avenging morality of nature. The only unique qualities in the story, in view of Sinclair's previous writings, are the descriptions of vicious economic and working conditions in "Hungryville." Almost everything else would be ludicrous even in a soap opera.

Sinclair later said that A *Captain of Industry* was the first fruit of his Socialistic point of view. If so, it seems that he took from Socialism only a keener interest in the evils of self-indulgence, sex, and money among the American plutocracy. Yet, as his next novel, *Manassas,* clearly reveals, Socialism also marked the beginning of Sinclair's intense and extensive interest in the problems of history and in the concrete world outside the idealist's consciousness.

VII Manassas

Sometime early in 1903 Sinclair began formulating plans to write a neo-abolitionist novel of the Civil War—a great American subject which he felt had gone untouched by a serious novelist. (Apparently, he had failed to read either *The Red Badge of Courage* or John William De Forest's excellent 1867 novel, *Miss Ravenel's Conversion.*) Although he did not intend to interpret the war in a strict Socialistic manner, his shift to the historical novel, a more objective form of fiction than he had been producing, and to an interest in the direction of historical change was certainly related to his new Socialist awareness. By writing a novel of the war and assuming in the process the ideological mantle of abolitionism, Sinclair could free himself of his essentially conservative Southern roots. Furthermore, by understanding fully the effectiveness and truth of abolitionism in the past, he could then step into a new and equally effective role as a propagandist for Socialism, heir of the spirit if not the ideology of the abolitionists.

Sinclair first contemplated a three volume work, to be entitled *The American,* dealing with the "monster" of "Rebellion" and stressing the necessity of saving the union at all costs. To finance such an ambitious writing venture, he had counted on royalties from *Arthur Stirling.* But when his hoax was discovered by reviewers and his book savaged, for instance, as "vulgar and impudent humbug,"[21] he arranged instead to borrow thirty dollars a month from George D. Herron until he could publish the first volume of his work.

Fortunately, *Prince Hagen* was accepted for publication about this time. Feeling successful, Sinclair wrote for the *Independent* a signed essay entitled "My Cause" in which he claimed his victory over circumstances by saying, "I, Upton Sinclair, would-be singer and penniless rat, having for seven years waged day and night with society a life-and-death struggle for the existence of my soul; and having now definitely and irrevocably consummated a victory. . . ."[22] He also tried to explain why he wrote *The Journal of Arthur Stirling* as he did; he explained the goals of his historical work; he stated a wish to establish "The Sinclair Press" to publish his own work and thus free it forever from commercialism; and he pledged himself to the founding of an "American University of Literature" to dispense funds to promising and needy writers like himself. After publishing "My Cause" in the spring of 1903, he moved himself and his family to a location near Princeton, New Jersey, where he would have access to the Civil War materials in the Princeton University Library.

He spent over a year writing his novel. At first he, Meta, and David lived in a tent in the New Jersey woods. Then in the fall of 1903 he built a cabin, where the family weathered an extremely harsh winter. Throughout this time Meta was generally depressed and miserable, and Sinclair found it difficult to reconcile his husbandly and fatherly duties with his literary labors, to which he often devoted sixteen hours a day. (In 1910 he made this New Jersey experience the core of his autobiographical novel, *Love's Pilgrimage.*) In spite of such problems, he completed his manuscript in May of 1904 and sent it off to the Macmillan Company, where it was readily accepted for publication. Since his story climaxed in the first battle of Bull Run, he called it *Manassas*. He hoped to complete the other volumes of his projected trilogy later.

Though far from a great work, *Manassas* (reprinted in 1959 as *Theirs Be the Guilt*) is Sinclair's best novel prior to *The Jungle*. In writing it he took many of the important historical facts related to the origins of the Civil War and worked them into a plot intended to resurrect the spirit of abolitionism. The theme he stressed was the almost holy Northern idealism which in the 1850's stood in shameful contrast to the slavery and greed in the South. Sinclair's observations of American life at the turn of the century apparently suggested that the nation had lost the ideals for which hundreds of thousands had died in the war. He prefaced his novel with the explanation "That the men of this land may know the heritage that is come down to them."[23] *Manassas* reflects a search for historical tradition in which many American reformers engaged prior to World War I.[24]

Sinclair later said that the real protagonist of *Manassas* is the Republic itself and that the novel was written in the spirit of Frank Norris's *The Octopus*.[25] Sinclair's novel vaguely resembles Norris's in its use of a culminating historical event—the battle of Bull Run—as a climax. Yet unlike *The Octopus*, it deals chiefly with the adventures of one character, Allan Montague, whose exploits involve an unusual number of historical events and persons. Montague, whose son is the main character in two later novels, was obviously the prototype of Lanny Budd, the peripatetic hero of Sinclair's historical novels during the 1940's.

Manassas is based on a conflict between Southern roots and nationalistic traditions. Although Allan Montague is the son of a Mississippi planter—and knows Jefferson Davis as a neighbor—he has Northern connections. His mother, who is deceased when the story begins, was the daughter of a prominent Boston family. His grandfather, who is still alive at the beginning of the novel, is a hero of the Revolutionary War and a tutor of patriotism. Furthermore, Allan has the good fortune to be sent to Boston for his education. There he reads *Uncle Tom's Cabin*, hears Frederick Douglass speak, and develops abolitionist sentiments. When he is eighteen, in 1856, he returns to Mississippi, where he helps free a Negro who has been illegally charged as a runaway. Fortunately, his father dies in a carriage accident before he can learn of his son's transgression of Southern values. Next, Allan returns to Boston, meets prominent abolitionist leaders, travels to meet John Brown, and manages to be present as a spectator at Harper's Ferry. He returns once more to Mississippi in an attempt to take possession of property that is rightfully his. However, he fails, is disowned by his relatives, and heads north as the war begins. He is present at the firing on Fort Sumter. In Washington, abolitionist friends introduce him to William Seward and Charles Francis Adams. He even converses with Lincoln. Finally, he joins a Massachusetts company and participates in the ill-fated first battle of Bull Run. His story ends as he observes his Mississippi cousins, now in the Confederate Army, celebrating their victory.

The quality of Sinclair's fiction in *Manassas* is not satisfying. Whole chapters of historical facts related by an omniscient narrator do little to advance the story of Allan Montague. Descriptions of both action and thought rely heavily on clichés and are strongly reminiscent of Sinclair's hack work. The characterization of Allan lacks complexity: he is an overly unselfish person who is never tempted by self-indulgence and for whom sex apparently has no existence. A greater flaw in the novel is produced by the remarkable incidents and coincidences of the plot which tend to destroy the credibility of the story. Its redeeming qualities are Sinclair's attempts to give life to figures like John Brown and Jefferson Davis, and his brutal descriptions of combat where, for example, Allan sees the head of a companion completely blown off.

As history the novel deserves more appreciation. Even though it is incredibly biased and inhabited by stereotypes, it often indicates the kind of false image that each section of the nation had of the other in the 1850's. Southerners in the story continually bewail the restrictions placed on them by an industrial North, and Northern abolitionists seem obsessed with the idea that slaves are treated with intentional cruelty. Although Sinclair at times suggests that abolitionists are motivated more by morality than by a deeply felt concern for slaves, he allows Allan to see that the real problem is the South: but it is less slavery *per se* than the lack of an advanced civilization. Slavery, acquisitiveness, irrationality, and immorality— not to mention the resulting economic effects on the entire nation— seem to be mere symptoms of an underlying malaise which must be treated, even if the therapy is war, in order for the Republic to stand.

As far as Sinclair's career is concerned, *Manassas* was a crucial book. The writing of it was more than a personal crusade against his own Southern roots and, by extension, his Southern father. It was also a means of adopting attitudes necessary to his later activities as a muckraker. By 1904 Sinclair had sensed the connection between the earlier anti-slavery crusade and the Progressive movement, of which Socialism was the most outspoken aspect. Soon he would be claiming the imminence of a Third American Revolution, the previous two having been waged for national political autonomy and for the emancipation of slaves. In a sense, *Manassas* was Upton Sinclair's rite of passage into American radicalism. The next move of his career was from ideology and principle to the hard facts of human exploitation in the economic jungle of Chicago's Packingtown.

CHAPTER 3

The Jungle

SINCLAIR's early novels emphasized imagination rather than reality and tended towards the sentimental or artificial. *Springtime and Harvest* was rightly subtitled "A Romance" *Prince Hagen* was "A Phantasy"; and *The Overman* was fantastical. *A Captain of Industry* dealt with contemporaneous material but depended upon an extraordinarily coincidental plot. *Manassas,* while making use of historical facts, was also excessive in its manipulation of plot and character, a kind of magic lantern of Civil War places and personalities. When *The Jungle* appeared in 1906 it represented a change in both the nature and quality of Sinclair's literary efforts.

Sinclair's most famous novel was based on the hard and undeniable facts of working-class life in the Chicago packing plant district. It had direct reference to contemporary politics, was largely the result of first-hand observation, and had a specific audience—the Socialists—whose political attitudes were largely shared with the author. In the end, *The Jungle* transcended political boundaries and reached a much wider audience—one of international proportions—but Sinclair's achievement was possible primarily by virtue of his Socialist involvement in 1904 and 1905. If the act of writing *Manassas* was a necessary ritual in Sinclair's ideological conversion to radicalism, *The Jungle* was a full expression of faith, an intense personal attempt to bring modern Socialism into literature and thereby fuse it with the narrative and empathetic powers of fiction.

I *Preparations*

By the time *Manassas* was finished in May of 1904, Sinclair had apparently decided against finishing his Civil War triology. Between the completion of *Manassas* and the beginning of research for *The*

44

Jungle in November of the same year, he spent most of his available time in two Socialist oriented tasks: reading about theoretics and philosophy, and developing an audience by writing pieces for mass circulation journals. At this time and throughout the twelve to fourteen months of researching and writing *The Jungle*, Socialism dominated Sinclair's existence—not only as a compelling ideology and literary material but also as a career and an identity. Yet, as in the past, Sinclair continued to suffer from a lack of money and from marital tensions.

The *Appeal to Reason*, a weekly Populistic-Socialistic journal published in Kansas by Julius Augustus Wayland since 1895, was a contributing factor in the writing of *The Jungle*. With an established circulation in the hundreds of thousands, the *Appeal* was the nation's foremost Socialist voice. It was also evidence of the agrarian and Western nature of the Socialist movement. By 1904, Sinclair was a conscientious reader of the *Appeal* and that year he also became one of its regular contributors. The pages of the *Appeal* provided Sinclair with his first real sense of the masses of workers and farmers who were the foundation of American Socialism. His own involvement with the movement had been restricted to a few members of the intellectual elite, and most of his own Socialistic expressions up to 1904 had been based on something other than contact with working-class life. Not only did the *Appeal* help provide the missing contact but it also identified Sinclair's future audience.

Through the *Appeal*'s reviews and articles Sinclair learned of such standard Socialist authors as Karl Kautsky, the German popularizer of Marx, Peter Kropotkin, the Russian critic of Darwinian social theory, and Jack London, the charismatic literary figure whose books and speeches were exciting Socialists throughout the world. It is tempting to play up such models and influences. However, the central role of the *Appeal* in Sinclair's career was that of introducing him to a large and sympathetic audience. From 1904 on, Sinclair aimed most of his writing at the kind of people who read this publication.

During the summer of 1904 Sinclair also became an official member of the Socialist Party of America. The first fruit of his membership was a series of articles in the *Appeal* concerning an unsuccessful strike in the Chicago meat packing industry that summer.[1] These articles—the first he had ever written specifically for working-class readers—informed readers that the Beef Trust was hardly amenable to union demands under the present capitalist system and that Socialism was an absolute necessity. These articles were also the inspiration for *The Jungle*.

At the same time *Manassas*, in spite of poor sales, was reaping a harvest of good reviews. The favorable reception of the novel among reviewers gave Sinclair sufficient publicity to gain access to the non-Socialist pages of *Collier's*, which published two of his articles in October of 1904. One was an explanation of the aims of the Socialist Party in the present election: to educate Americans about social injustice and to thereby pave the way for economic democracy, and to avoid revolution.[2] The other article, "Our Bourgeois Literature," was ostensibly a response to a piece by Gertrude Atherton in the *North American Review* calling American literature "timid," "anemic," and "bourgeois." In the context of Sinclair's career, the article was a personal reassessment of the relationship between the artist and his society.

Sinclair agreed with Atherton's criticism of American literature but could not find adequate proof of its timid qualities in her essay. The kind of bourgeois expression she described, he said, was actually the result and fault of a bourgeois society. After all, he pointed out, "there can be no soul-life for any man until it is for all, . . . there can be among us neither political virtue, nor social refinement, nor true religion, nor vital art, so long as men, women, and little children are chained up to toil for us in mines and factories and sweatshops, are penned in filthy slums, and fed upon offal, and doomed to rot and perish in soul-sickening misery and horror."[3]

In this serious statement, Sinclair insists that society must change before art can, that art, rather than transcending the social structure, depends upon it. By implication, Sinclair also commits the artist to social change not only for the sake of society but for the sake of encouraging "vital art." Two years earlier, in *Prince Hagen*, Sinclair had said that artists, the "soul" of society, are to blame for America's problems. By 1904, on the eve of his involvement with *The Jungle*, Sinclair had come to realize that society should be blamed for the failure of art.

With this realization, Sinclair could now direct his efforts away from the idealistic writing that characterized his earlier novels towards literature that would help alleviate the conditions of life under capitalism. To repair American culture from the bottom up, he had to deal specifically with lower-class life and practical politics. At the time "Our Bourgeois Literature" was published, Sinclair was already thinking about a novel of lower-class life. His initial inspiration was the unsuccessful Chicago strike that he had described in the *Appeal*. As early as October of 1904 he was proposing to George P. Brett, his editor at Macmillan (publishers of *Manassas*), a new novel which "would be intended to set forth the breaking of human hearts by a system which exploits the labor of men and women for profits." Furthermore, this work "would be a definite attempt to do something popular" rather than the kind of "artistic work" he had been writing.[4]

Sinclair's plans for such a novel were initially encouraged by Brett—and eventually by a five hundred dollar advance from Macmillan. But Sinclair was more impressed by the encouragement from Fred D. Warren, editor of the *Appeal to Reason*, who challenged him to write a novel as good as *Manassas* but dealing with present-day wage slavery instead of chattel slavery. Warren offered five hundred dollars for the serial rights to such a novel. Sinclair quickly accepted and made plans for a trip to Chicago, where he felt certain he would find the material he needed for his novel. In short order he made a down payment on a small New Jersey farm, moved Meta and David there, and, in early November of 1904, set off for Packingtown.

The Jungle grew out of the personal impressions and factual information that Sinclair gathered for about seven weeks. This investigation was not especially long, but Sinclair did his work well, devoting practically all of his waking hours to the task. Although he was essentially an outsider, he interviewed laborers, social workers, lawyers, doctors, saloonkeepers, and others who seemed to know anything about conditions in the packing plants and political corruption in Chicago. His status as a Socialist won him the confidence of workers who invited him into their homes for interviews that detailed the filth and danger that existed in the plants. Sinclair was also careful to tour the packing plants in two ways: as an official visitor and as a disguised worker. What he saw sickened him. Although he must have been prepared mentally to see the worst—having written previously about workers "doomed to rot and perish in soul-sickening misery and horror"—his experience at Packingtown made a traumatic, life-long impression on him. What World War I meant to Ernest Hemingway, what the experiences of poverty and crime meant to Jack London, the combination of visible oppression and underlying corruption in Chicago in 1904 meant to Upton Sinclair. *This* kind of evidence, *this* kind of commitment to social justice became the primal experience of his fiction. For at least the next four decades, beginning with *The Jungle*, Sinclair would continually retell the story of what happened to him in Chicago.

In December, Sinclair returned to New Jersey. Working at his typically compulsive rate, he began to transform his information and emotions into a novel. The task was formidable. He had to achieve a realistic portrayal of a way of life—the immigrant worker's—that was alien to his own background and experience, and to express his story in such a way as to make a persuasive case for Socialism.

Sinclair spent most of 1905 writing his novel. In his first public statement of intention, published in the *Appeal* two weeks before the novel began as a serial, he expanded what he had earlier described to George P. Brett. *The Jungle*, he said, "will set forth the breaking of human hearts by a system which exploits the labor of men and women for profits. It will shake the popular heart and blow the roof off of the industrial tea-kettle. What Socialism there will be in this book, will, of course, be imminent; it will be revealed by incidents—there will be no sermons. The novel will not have any superficial resemblance to 'Uncle Tom's Cabin.' Fundamentally it will be identical with it—or try to be."[5]

The confident tone of this statement indicates that Sinclair's original intentions were holding firm and that the writing had progressed smoothly. He had known for months that the 1904 Chicago strike would be a major event in his story. He also knew his setting and had decided that his main character was to be a Lithuanian named Jurgis Rudkus who resembled a worker he had observed at a wedding feast in Packingtown. Furthermore, in imagining the oppressiveness of his characters' lives, he was aided by his own experiences of poverty, by Meta's illnesses, and by the bitter cold he and his family had endured the previous winter. Even as he worked on his novel he complained to Macmillan of having to devote much time to Meta, who was continually under medical care.[6] The scenes of hunger, illness, cold, and fear in the novel, Sinclair later claimed, were parallel to his own experiences.[7] It is doubtful that anyone with a comfortable existence and a secure marital relationship could have written *The Jungle*.

Sinclair was also aided by the growing national concern over adulterated food. The characters he chose for his novel were, after all, workers in packing plants, and he had personally observed the unsanitary processes by which meat was packed. For years, beginning with "embalmed meat" scandals during the Spanish-American

War, muckrakers had been criticizing the so-called Beef Trust, directing attention not only at unhealthy food but also at monopolistic business practices and corrupt political connections. Dr. Harvey W. Wiley, head of the Bureau of Chemistry in the Department of Agriculture, had also been publicizing the ill effects of additives in meat products and demanding national legislation to insure pure food. While he was in Chicago, Sinclair interviewed a correspondent for the *Lancet*, the prominent British medical journal, who provided him with detailed information about slaughterhouse conditions. Whether Sinclair knew it or not—and he probably did—he was dealing with a subject of vital interest to all Americans, Socialist or not.

In spite of its confident tone, Sinclair's announcement in the *Appeal* identified the chief difficulty that he faced in the later stages of writing *The Jungle*. Committed first of all to a naturalistic story about the "breaking of human hearts," he also wanted to promote Socialism as a way of preventing any future heartbreaking. Furthermore, he felt that his political message could be expressed through the "incidents" of his plot rather than through authorial "sermons." As he said later, *The Jungle* attempted to "put the content of Shelley into the form of Zola."[8] That his political idealism was doomed to contradict his naturalism—that Shelley and Zola might be fundamentally incompatible—apparently did not cross Sinclair's mind early in 1905.

II *Results*

The naturalism that Sinclair wanted to achieve came easily. In the first twenty-one chapters (out of thirty-one in the final version published by Doubleday in 1906) he wrote a kind of *Uncle Tom's Cabin* of wage slavery, without including Mrs. Stowe's awareness of spiritual redemption (or perhaps substituting it with Socialist redemption). His novel details the experience of one wage slave and his family who, like Uncle Tom, accept an unjust social system that they cannot escape. The story of Jurgis Rudkus and his Lithuanian relatives in this part of the novel follows the classic naturalistic pattern of inexorable movement towards chaos and doom. Lured from Europe by the American dream of success, they arrive in Packingtown filled with hope, follow all the rules of frugality and hard work, but eventually become the victims of an acquisitive society. In the economic jungle of lower-class American life, all paths apparently lead to the destruction of life and spirit.

The Jungle begins with the *vesilija*, the feast after the wedding of
Jurgis Rudkus and Ona Lukoszaite, a traditional ceremony which
illustrates the desperate desire for order and community on the part
of the Lithuanian immigrants who are struggling to make a living in
Packingtown. But the old ways have already been destroyed by
American life. Older men and women in particular feel the corrupting power of the new world in which they must live, an industrial
realm of wages and hours and profit quite different from the bucolic
world of their past. Young people now dance in shocking new ways,
and many refuse to pay their share of the *vesilija* expenses. It is "as if
there must be some subtle poison in the air that one breathed
here—it was affecting all the young men at once."[9] Rather than
accept their responsibility to the whole group, the young men eat,
drink, and then leave the feast without volunteering to pay a cent,
often even "staring at you, and making fun of you to your face" (20).
Towards the end of the *vesilija*, the participants—who by now are
weary with exhaustion and with the prospects of going back to work in
a few hours—find themselves hypnotized by the popular American
tune, "In the Good Old Summer Time." "No one can get away from
it, or even think of getting away from it" (24). They are all saddened
when they realize the discrepancy between the actual and the
possible in America.

The consciousness of Sinclair's proletarian hero is initially a matter
of assumed possibilities which eventually become mere illusions.
Jurgis Rudkus is different from the irresponsible young men at the
feast. He is a staunch individual, prized for his strength and his ability
to work, who happily accepts his responsibility to others. He has
come to America, "a place of which lovers and young people
dreamed" (27), as the leader of a group of twelve Lithuanians
including his father, Ona, and a number of Ona's relatives. His roots
are strictly agrarian: before his journey to Packingtown he had never
seen a city. He. is a strong believer in the ethic of work and his
standard reply to problems is "I will work harder." Although Sinclair
reveals that Jurgis comes to America with no understanding of the
prevailing language, he never has him speak in dialect. Nor does he
emphasize his Catholic faith. From the beginning of the novel Jurgis
seems almost indigenously American, a stereotype of the American
dreamer in search of success in the form of enough wealth to get
married, live without great insecurity, and take care of his relatives.

Jurgis scrupulously follows the American dream and the ethic of
work. When he takes up the life of a wage slave in Packingtown he

begins by admiring the genius of American capitalism, even accepting the great packing plant as a universe in itself and the process of
packing meat as "a wonderful poem" (41). He also accepts the
standard laissez-faire attitude towards labor: when other workers
complain about the speeding up of the butchering process, Jurgis
knows that he can perform at the accelerated rate and thinks that
others could too "if they were good for anything" (62). At home, being
a good family man, Jurgis conscientiously arranges to buy a house for
his and Ona's families before he agrees to marriage. A man of
patience, he even postpones his wedding for sixteen months in order
to provide security for the Lithuanian tribe. After he gets a job by
being selected from a crowd of men on the basis of his commanding
physical presence, he buys a home and marries Ona; he also goes to
night school to learn English and soon becomes an American citizen.
But all of these attempts at success fail. For Jurgis the American
dream and the ethic of work become a nightmare of effort without
reward.

Sinclair indicates that Jurgis's striving is mostly in vain. Material
success is impossible because the Packingtown workers are the slaves
of the capitalist packers who grow fatter and more prosperous as the
workers grow hungrier and poorer. At least for Jurgis the hope of
upward mobility is a chimera. Furthermore, he and the rest of the
wage slaves are kept from a meaningful community life by the
struggle for mere existence. In Sinclair's Packingtown there is little
sense of solidarity or of people engaged in any kind of social
intercourse. Saloons, unions, and perhaps whorehouses are possibilities, but the novel indicates that they offer only a false sense of
community. All that union members can do, for instance, is stage
unsuccessful strikes and gather together "to discuss the election of a
recording secretary" (92). Schools, churches, settlement houses, and
relief societies have no real function in Sinclair's industrial jungle.

Jurgis's adventures as a well-intentioned, responsible, and social
man are therefore a catalogue of tragedies. First, every able-bodied
member of his family must work. Then his father dies and Jurgis can
shamefully afford only a cheap funeral. Ona bears him a child, a boy
whom he names Antanas after his father, but since Ona must return
immediately to work she, like Meta Sinclair, soon develops "womb
trouble" and suffers greatly thereafter. Although he works manfully
at his job on the killing beds at the packing plant, when he turns an
ankle and spends weeks convalescing, Jurgis loses his job. Un-
daunted, however, he finds a position at a fertilizer plant. This new job

is the worst imaginable employment, for it requires him to breathe bone dust and absorb the odors of animal remains; but he accepts it as his duty to his wife and family. His pay is poor, and Ona must clandestinely prostitute herself to keep the family going. When Jurgis discovers her "sacrifice," he rushes out in a blind rage to attack the man who forced Ona into prostitution. His act of violence lands him in jail for thirty days. When he is released he discovers to his dismay that his house, obviously a symbol of the family's stability, has been repossessed. He finds his family only to see Ona die of a miscarriage in a powerful scene of pain and horror. Feeling deeply guilty for what has happened to her, he continues to accept responsibility as head of the household and locates new work, first in a harvester plant and then in a steel mill. But upon returning from work one day he finds that little Antanas has drowned in the rain water standing in the unpaved streets of Packingtown.

Throughout the early chapters of the novel, Sinclair is explicit not only about the pain and oppression that his immigrant characters suffer, but also about the horrors of meat packing which they must helplessly watch. The immigrants are also exposed to the corrupt nature of politics in a community where elections are never less than a fraud, and to the economic stranglehold exerted by the Beef Trust and its lackeys.

The narrative that Sinclair produced in his first twenty-one chapters was not, however, all that he wanted to do. He still faced the problem of ending his story on a note of Socialist hope. The problem was both ideological and literary. It was certainly appropriate from the standpoint of Socialist ideas for him to show how capitalism crushed the lives of workers; but Sinclair's personal optimism would not let him leave matters at this point. He was obligated to show his readers how the workers would eventually overcome capitalist oppression. Yet by the time he began to end his novel, after spending twenty chapters without really suggesting that his Packingtown victims were part of a larger and hopeful historical or economic movement, it would have been difficult to reveal the solution of Socialism without vitiating the plot that *Appeal* readers had been following. In Emile Zola's *Germinal*, which Sinclair apparently had in mind as a model, the French naturalist avoided Sinclair's problems by creating a story of wage slavery climaxing in a abortive uprising of French coal miners which, in spite of its failure, allowed the protagonist—but not Zola himself—to claim that the miners "had shaken the workers of all France by their cry for justice." Zola unified this story by using a central character, Etienne Lantier, who is first involved in the mining community and who later leads the uprising. This solution was not possible for Sinclair. In the first place, he would not have considered using an Americanized version of Zola's plot. Secondly, his central character is in no condition to become a Socialist leader after his many tragedies as a Packingtown worker.

Sinclair's attempt to bring Socialism into the plot depended therefore on first raising Jurgis's consciousness—on turning him into something besides a pathetic follower of the work ethic. Earlier in the novel, Jurgis deviates from the work ethic temporarily by drinking to dull the pain of his existence. After the death of his son in chapter twenty-one, the characterization of Jurgis becomes much more rebellious, though his rebellion is entirely undirected. He becomes a tramp, a burglar, a political henceman, and a strikebreaker.

Chapter twenty-two is particularly significant. Antanas's death is the last straw for Jurgis. Seized by a "wild impulse," he swings himself onto a freight car and heads for the countryside determined never again to feel tenderness, never again to accept responsibility for anyone except himself, never again to fall prey to regret and sorrow. He rebels against both the kind of society in which he has tried to live, and his own compassion. After he leaves the city, Jurgis wanders in the country, refuses to take a steady job, and hopes to avoid thinking about his past. As soon as possible he finds a stream and bathes thoroughly, as if he could scour off not only the dirt and grease of his life as a wage slave but also the memory of his family. Afterwards, guided by "wanderlust" in his blood, he seeks the "joy of the unbound life, the joy of seeking, of hoping without limit" (215). He regains health and feels for awhile as if his childhood has returned. But his individualistic joy is an illusion, for his vagabond life soon leads, by way of money earned in the harvest fields, to saloons and whorehouses where his "wild rioting and debauchery" stimulate pangs of conscious and memory. Within him a "tomb of memory" opens, and he realizes that in his life outside society he is "writhing and suffocating in the mire of his own vileness" (217–19). The extent of his anomie is indicated when he destroys a whole row of young peach trees in a farmer's orchard.

Jurgis returns to Chicago the following autumn. He finds a job digging tunnels beneath the city but discovers that the wages and security of a job are no protection against loneliness. The single life is not good and he has no place to go in the evenings except to saloons: "He had now no home to go to; he had no affection left in his life—only the pitiful mockery of it in the comraderie of vice" (222). Here Sinclair seems to indicate that family life has meaning even under capitalism; at the very least it is a stay against the bottle and the whorehouse.

In the city Jurgis continues to discover the perils of life outside the bonds of community. When an accident injures him and forces him out of his job, he takes up begging on the streets where he runs into the drunken son of a wealthy meat packer. Jurgis learns that the money of the rich does not lead to happiness any more than does the poverty of the worker: Freddie Jones, the packer's son, reveals that wealth produces only banality, dissipation, and a loveless family life based on status and social expectations. After this enlightening encounter, Jurgis becomes a burglar; burglary leads to political connections and to a position as a ward heeler for the Democratic machine in Packingtown. When a strike erupts in the plants, the strike that had been the original inspiration for the novel, Jurgis sees his opportunity for a good job after the packers break the strike, and he goes to work as a strikebreaker along with "a throng of stupid black Negroes and foreigners" (266). During the strike he observes "a saturnalia of debauchery" because for the first time in their lives the Negroes are free—"free to gratify every passion, free to wreck themselves" (270). This kind of statement, clearly racist in its implications, seems to embody Sinclair's belief that without the restraints of an orderly and just society freedom is dangerous—as is the freedom provided by excess wealth.

During the strike Jurgis runs into Phil Connor, the man who had coerced Ona into prostitution a year earlier. Unable to restrain his anger, he attacks Connor for a second time; and for a second time he is thrown into jail. When he is released he encounters by chance one of the members of his family, Marija Berczynskas, Ona's cousin, who has taken up employment in a whorehouse. Marija tries to convince him that he was wrong in reacting as he did when he discovered that his wife was a prostitute: "Ona could have taken care of us all, in the beginning," she says (287). But Jurgis does not accept the argument. The idea of prostitution, which might provide material goods for the survival of the family as an economic unit but which would surely undermine its moral structure, only sickens him. As he leaves Marija, he thinks back upon the plight of his family. For a year he had successfully fought off sentiment. But now he hears "the old voices of his soul" and knows that if they "fade away into the mists of the past once more" then "the last faint spark of manhood in his soul would flicker out" (290). His problem, one of the major problems that Sinclair explores in the novel, is how to keep from losing his manhood—his concern for others—in a social and economic system which continually transforms concern into helplessness and sorrow.

At this point Jurgis finally discovers Socialism. He stumbles into a political meeting after leaving Marija, and after a while he begins to listen to the speaker, who tells "a story of hope and freedom." The speaker, combining the qualities of Eugene V. Debs and George D. Herron, says that his words can open his listeners' eyes, thus "solving all problems, making all difficulties clear," by revealing the greed of a pitifully few wealthy capitalists who exploit the labor of the rest of humanity (299). Such statements are news to Jurgis, and as he listens to them he experiences what can be described only as a religious conversion to Socialism. When the Socialist lecture is over, Jurgis knows "that in the mighty upheaval that had taken place in his soul, a new man had been born" (304). He is now free from the bondage of ignorance and the compliance with evil which had been his lot since the death of his son. Furthermore, looking upward from the proletariat, he realizes now that there are "men who would show him and help him; and he would have friends and allies, he would dwell in the sight of justice, and walk arm in arm with power" (304).

Sinclair had real difficulty in deciding when and how to introduce Socialism. By the summer of 1905 he had apparently finished his story up to Jurgis's experiences with the packer's son. This much of *The Jungle* was published by J. A. Wayland, publisher of the *Appeal*, in *One Hoss Philosophy* (another Populist-Socialist magazine) in July. No more of the story appeared until October.[10] In September, Sinclair was enthusiastically involved in founding the Intercollegiate Socialist Society (later the League for Industrial Democracy). This effort introduced him to many prominent Socialist leaders, including Jack London, and conceivably convinced him of the importance of getting Socialism into his plot even if he had to do it with sermons. Whereas Sinclair's experiences in Packingtown may be seen as the inspiration for the naturalistic part of *The Jungle*, his involvement with the Socialist elite—few if any being wage slaves—may be seen as the source of the last four chapters in which Socialism is offered as an answer to the problems of wage slavery.

Sinclair finally presents Socialistic concepts in the closing chapters of his novel as part of a radical morality play in which the hero comes to accept as sinful the way in which he has worked unresistingly and individualistically within the capitalist system. In Socialism, Jurgis rediscovers his manhood: it is the only possible way for him to regain his concern for others, his belief in the family, and his intuitive understanding of social justice. After his conversion, after he loses his faith in competition, he returns to live with the remainder of his family—Ona's step-mother and her children. Once he becomes a Socialist, he is also able to obtain a job working as a porter for a Socialist hotel owner. Above all, he can once again allow himself to accept responsibility and feel sentiment.

In the sequence of events following Jurgis's discovery of Socialism, Sinclair was able to introduce the light of political hope into the darkness of Packingtown. But in so doing, he also shifted the focus of his novel from Jurgis to the Socialist movement itself. Up to his accidental stumbling into the Socialist lecture, Jurgis's story is almost entirely his own, and is powerful in Sinclair's heart-breaking way. In the last chapters of the novel, however, Jurgis becomes only a fictional device which allows Sinclair to introduce political propaganda and theory in the form of speeches and conversations. In the final chapter, for instance, Jurgis listens to a dialogue between an "itinerant evangelist" named Lucas, who believes that the Socialist revolution will be an essentially religious movement based on the teachings of Jesus, and a Swedish professor and "scientific" revolutionary theoretician named Schliemann. Schliemann, who dominates the dialogue, pictures a Socialist utopia in which machines do most of man's labor and in which society is organized more or less according to the plan in Edward Bellamy's *Looking Backward.* The final scene of the novel also pays scant attention to Jurgis. At a rally following the 1904 election—with Socialist gains clearly evident—another orator announces, in the famous last four words of the novel, that "CHICAGO WILL BE OURS!"

There is some evidence that Sinclair was not completely happy with this ending. In the final *One Hoss Philosophy* version, which appeared in October of 1905 (some three months before the book version) Jurgis is arrested at the election rally because he has jumped bail after being arrested for assaulting Phil Connor the second time. The triumphant results of the 1904 election are then followed by a statement indicating that Jurgis was on his way to prison. This ending, however, with its final naturalistic jab at social injustice in America, was omitted in favor of the more cheerful finish of the book version.[11]

In the end Sinclair was not able to carry out his intentions of a heart-breaking story with imminent Socialism. Instead he settled for an uneven story dealing mainly with proletarian experience until the last four chapters, which switch disturbingly to the Socialist movement, its leaders, and its ideas. There are various explanations for this shift that weakens the novel. Leon Harris, in his biography of Sinclair, says that the young writer "found himself paralyzed; for the first time in his life he was unable to write" as he tried to complete *The Jungle* in 1905.[12] Also, since he was then suffering severe marital and financial problems, he may have rushed to a conclusion in what seemed to be the only way at the time. As mentioned before, he was also probably enthralled with the idea of sermonistic Socialism as a result of his activities with the Intercollegiate Socialist Society. But, given the magnitude of his intentions, his own explanation may be quite sufficient: "I did the best I could."[13]

III   *The Rhetoric of Food*

The Jungle was eventually published by Doubleday, Page, and Company in 1906 after Macmillan decided that many of its scenes—especially those in the packing plants—were possibly libelous. Doubleday confirmed Sinclair's facts by sending investigators to Chicago, however, and advertised the novel as "a searching exposé of . . . the flagrant violations of all hygienic laws in the slaughter of diseased cattle . . . and the whole machinery of feeding a nation."[14] This kind of advertisement may have omitted Sinclair's original intentions—to write a searching exposé of wage slavery—but by capitalizing on the growing public furor over contaminated food, it helped make *The Jungle* a best seller and its author a world-famous writer. Furthermore, the success of *The Jungle* as a muckraking novel about food processing (rather than a Socialist novel about wage slavery) propelled Sinclair into active reform politics during 1906. He pleaded with President Roosevelt to order an investigation of sanitary conditions in the Chicago plants, and he agitated for passage of the Pure Food and Drug Bill that had been stalled for months in Congress. In June the bill finally became law, *The Jungle* being a major contributing factor to its passage.

In view of the novel's impact as a muckraking story about the nation's food, no analysis of *The Jungle* should avoid Sinclair's treatment of meat and its processing. Simply in terms of what it did to national eating patterns, the novel was a rhetorical achievement of remarkable dimensions. According to Waverly Root and Richard de Rochemont in *Eating in America*, Sinclair's presentation of unsanitary practices in the meat industry prevented Americans from regaining their appetite for meat—or at least for meat processed by packing houses—for several decades. In 1928, the packers were still campaigning for Americans to "eat more meat."[15] Readers of *The Jungle* were not yet able to buy meat products with a clear conscience. An obvious case in point is Sinclair's claim that some workers fell into cooking vats, "and when they were fished out, there was never enough of them to be worth exhibiting—sometimes they would be overlooked for days, till all but the bones of them had gone out to the world as Durham's Pure Leaf Lard!" (102). If it was not workers in the lard that shocked the nation in 1906, it was the chemicals, the rat dung, and the assortment of other putrid substances that Sinclair pictured as ending up in the stomachs of American consumers.

Shortly after the novel appeared Sinclair claimed that actually he had not been much concerned with meat processing when he wrote his story. His often quoted statement to this effect—"I aimed at the public's heart, and by accident I hit it in the stomach"—has considerable validity to it.[16] His initial motivation had been the failure of the 1904 strike in the Chicago stockyards, and his concern from the beginning had doubtless been the conditions under which the wage slaves of industry were forced to work and live. Furthermore, the amount of space in the novel that is actually devoted to documenting sanitation in the packing plants is small; in fact, Jurgis leaves the plants well before *The Jungle* is half finished. Yet in spite of such facts, and of the greater purpose of the novel, Sinclair did intend to hit America in the stomach. If anything, the punch was premeditated—and well-aimed.

The intentional focus on matters of the stomach in the novel may be illustrated in several ways. The use of footnotes to present direct quotations from Department of Agriculture regulations concerning the inspection of intrastate meat (98) shows Sinclair's willingness to interrupt the flow of his story, mixing nonfiction with fiction, for the sake of authoritative documentation and, eventually, pure meat. Such facts of meat inspection did not directly affect the lives of oppressed workers who constituted Sinclair's expressed main interest. Middle-class readers would of course have recognized a direct effect on the meat they consumed. Sinclair's careful attention in *The Jungle* to questions like meat inspection provides a rather interesting contradiction of a second statement that he made at the time of his famous heart and stomach comment: "I do not eat meat myself, and my general attitude toward the matter was one of indifference."[17]

Other aspects of *The Jungle* hardly suggest indifference towards meat. Even the passage about workers who fall into the cooking vats directs attention mainly to ingredients in a consumer product. The real danger to the workers seems slighted; the agony of those who actually fall into the vats is not even mentioned. Chapter fourteen of the novel is another good example of a concern with food which seems in fact to precede his concern with the lives of his working-class characters. The main point of the chapter, which takes place midway through the story, is the accelerating deteriorioation of Jurgis's Lithuanian family after three years in Packingtown. By this time, according to Sinclair, after several deaths in the family and no relaxation of the vicious poverty in which they had been living: "They were beaten; they had lost the game, they were swept aside. It was not less tragic because it was so sordid, because that it had to do with wages and grocery bills and rents. They had dreamed of freedom; of a chance to look about them and learn something; to be decent and clean, to see their child grow up to be strong. And now it was gone—it would never be! They had played the game and they had lost" (137–38). Much of their story remained to be told—seventeen more chapters, in fact—but Sinclair wished in this early chapter to show the extent of their despair. Yet this chapter, with its deterministic emphasis on the inability of the workers to better their situation through their own efforts, begins not with an account of the troubles of the immigrants, nor even with the oppressiveness of the conditions under which they must work. Rather, Sinclair starts the chapter with several pages of exposition devoted to the subject of rotten hams and rat-adulterated sausage. For instance, he points out how no one ever pays the least attention to sausage ingredients: "there would come all the way back from Europe old sausage that had been rejected, and that was moldy and white—it would be dosed with borax and glycerine, and dumped into the hoppers, and made over again for home consumption." Or that "there were things that went into the sausage in comparison with which a poisoned rat was a tidbit" (136).

In other words, Sinclair apparently felt that the way to a reader's heart was through his stomach. Once the sickening facts of meat processing were served up, he could move on to the struggle for survival that his characters were inexorably losing.

The novel abounds with other instances of Sinclair's willingness to use his story of wage slavery and the soul-destroying jungle of capitalist exploitation as a vehicle for raking in the muck of adulterated food. The processing of "steerly" cattle which were covered with boils, of tubercular animals, or of cows about to calve; the use of tripe, pork fat, beef suet, and other non-poultry items to make "potted chicken"; the rechurning of rancid butter; the doctoring of milk with formaldehyde; and the cutting of ice from pools of stagnant and polluted water are among the examples. One can easily guess why a young and fervid Socialist writer at this time in America would take pains so often to attack food processing; his Socialism had an obvious middle-class bias to it. Although he spoke *for* the lowest working classes, he spoke *to* a much wider audience in *The Jungle*. (In fact, his vision of Socialist triumph was something to be achieved by majority vote, not an end result of class struggle and revolution. The statement that "Chicago will be ours!" at the end of the novel refers only to voting gains in the 1904 elections.) He wanted to show that not only did the Beef Trust exploit the lives of the workers, it also exploited the ignorance of the middle-class public. Food and its processing could therefore be used politically and rhetorically as a means of bridging class differences.

IV *Pictures of the Working Class*

As a work of modern fiction measured against the aesthetic achievements of a Henry James or a William Faulkner or a James Joyce, *The Jungle* hardly merits any discussion at all. Psychological complexity is alien to Sinclair's characterization, style is a matter of piling up details and modifiers, and structure is confused after the first twenty-one chapters. While such criticisms are common as well as obvious, they seem out of place, almost completely unrelated to the features of *The Jungle* that contribute to or detract from its significance and power.

The historical significance of *The Jungle* lies in Sinclair's attempt to bring working-class life into fiction without censoring any of the oppressiveness of that life as he observed it. Stephen Crane had, of course, dealt with the working class previously in *Maggie: A Girl of the Streets* and *George's Mother*, but his efforts had been directed towards a sophisticated effect of irony and impressionism. Numerous other writers had written of the lower class by imposing a cheerful optimism upon it; Horatio Alger's stories come to mind here. But Sinclair was uninterested in artistic effect and dubious of the American dream of success through individual pluck and luck. Instead, as Harvey Swados has aptly put it, he wanted to draw a vivid picture of "the cruelly used builders of the modern age," the industrial workers themselves.[18] Although Sinclair was a thorough

Progressive in his political and economic ideas, and chose to offer a virtual paean to progress in the words of "Herr Doctor" Schliemann at the end of his novel, *The Jungle* was his attempt to shout "Stop!" to uncontrolled industrial progress. The dehumanizing aspects of technological progress as he presents them are legion: the exploitation of immigrants, the cruelty of child labor, the artificial speeding up of human labor by machine processes, environmental pollution, slum life in industrial centers.

In simpler terms, *The Jungle* is a muckraking novel directed at documenting conditions and striving for an emotional response on the part of readers. In his novel Sinclair attacks traditional distinctions between literature and life. With *The Jungle* literature is less a way of ordering and interpreting experience—less the imposition of a particular artistic vision—than a way of simply presenting life and, in the subjective way that Sinclair does this, responding to it with regret, shame, and anger. Larzer Ziff, in his book on the rebellious literary generation of the 1890's, contrasts American literary expressions from 1901 to 1915 as reflecting "the calm of a pleasant senility."[19] *The Jungle* is an obvious exception to Ziff's generalization.

These comments should not imply that Sinclair's presentation of working-class life is completely or consistently radical. For instance, his treatment of adulterated food as a kind of middle-class rhetoric works against his lower-class focus. The novel also incorporates a tension between the attitudes of elitist culture and the facts of working-class life. Although this tension is mainly apparent in the closing chapters, it was to become a standard feature of Sinclair's novels. He was devoted to exposing the oppressive conditions of proletarian life under capitalism, and he apparently wrote with a working-class audience in mind. Yet he tended to view his lower-class subjects from elitist or genteel perspectives which were most likely the residual effects of his earlier idealism, his romantic fascination with Nietzsche, and the even earlier attitudes of his childhood and adolescence.

For example, *The Jungle* imposes traditional American images on its foreign characters. They have Lithuanian names, of course, but they do not seem noticeably alien in dialect, religion, and culture. Neither do they exhibit radical political ideas. Jurgis's own ideological convictions, which seldom reach the surface of his consciousness, are conservatively directed towards family responsibility and social order. Not until he loses his father, his wife, and his son to the capitalistic jungle does he become rebellious against society. Even then, his rebellion does not take a political form; it is merely purposeless and criminal. Such a picture of immigrant existence is undoubtedly a part of Sinclair's well-intentioned effort to destroy popular attitudes about foreigners as generally and even morally different from the white, Anglo-Saxon, and Protestant American image. Yet by refusing to see his characters in the terms of their own culture and ethnicity. Sinclair may have overcorrected the immigrant image.

When Jurgis becomes a Socialist by listening to the kind of sermons that Sinclair had hoped to avoid, the problem of depicting the immigrant working class reaches serious proportions. The first sermon, the one that transforms Jurgis's life from vagabondage and criminality to purpose and politics, arouses the following response in Jurgis's feelings: "A flood of emotion surged up in him—all his old hopes and longings, his old griefs and rages and despairs. All that he had ever felt in his whole life seemed to come back to him at once, and with one new emotion, hardly to be described"(303). The difficulty with this response lies in what it suggests about the way that Jurgis becomes a political radical. In the sequence of naturalistically depicted episodes preceding Jurgis's emotional conversion, Sinclair does not imply that the workers' own experiences will result in practical political action. The life of Jurgis Rudkus offers little foundation for radical politics. Sinclair's proletarians move directly from their naive dreams of success to degradation and anomie. In this way *The Jungle* suggests that the American working class at its lowest level is a vulnerable and easily destroyed culture. That class resembles black culture under slavery as it is sometimes described in neoabolitionist arguments, the ruling class having completely destroyed family structures and viable cultural resources. It seems somewhat ironic that Sinclair claimed that *The Jungle* would be fundamentally identical to *Uncle Tom's Cabin*. In Mrs. Stowe's novel Uncle Tom is capable of resisting the worst conditions of slavery without any real assistance outside his own black-rooted Christianity.

Jurgis apparently needs help. In the conversion scene he is actually made to feel guilty about what he has been and what he has done. The "one new emotion, hardly to be described" turns out to be rather well described as a consciousness of sin and an intense feeling of shame. Even as he listens to the rest of the oration Jurgis realizes the errors of his past. "That he should have suffered such horrors was bad enough; but that he should have been crushed and beaten by them, that he should have submitted, and forgotten, and lived in peace—ah, truly that was a thing not to be put into words, a thing not to be borne by a human creature, a thing of terror and madness!" (303). The rhetorical technique by which Jurgis enters the Socialist movement is that of Protestant evangelicalism. Little about it is proletarian; in fact, it depends largely on a rejection—a purging—of the proletarian experiences that came before it. What Mike Gold refers to as a "dark proletarian instinct which distrusts all that is connected with money-making"[20] has no role in *The Jungle*. Instead, in order for Jurgis to doubt capitalism he must be twice born—with the second birth being delivered by evangelical emotion.

The conversion chapter of *The Jungle* and the three that follow it comprise Sinclair's attempt to depict a redeemed order, a sort of kingdom of God on earth which will result from the conversion of almost everyone to Socialism (referred to as "the new gospel"). The industrial jungle gives way to a garden of technological delight. This turn of events moves the novel far away from the realistic scenes of earlier chapters and effectively eliminates Jurgis as the central interest of the narrative. For most of his story Sinclair presents proletarian life with due respect, often describing the immigrants and their surroundings from a point of view approximating their own. After Jurgis's conversion, however, Sinclair's attitudes towards his protagonist and the lower social class he represents seem to take on qualities of paternalism and condescension.[21] The orator who sends a flood of emotion surging up in Jurgis, for instance, speaks of capitalism being overcome by "the painful gropings of the *untutored* mind, by the *feeble* stammerings of the *uncultured* voice!" (302, emphasis added). The condescending choice of adjectives is reinforced by political implications. The overcoming of capitalism that the orator speaks of does not really seem to be the task of the working class. The responsibilities fall mainly on the shoulders of men like himself—articulate, educated, even wealthy spokesmen. These are the Socialists whom Jurgis comes to admire in the last four chapters of *The Jungle*. Of course, no one is planning a revolution. The closing words of the novel—"CHICAGO WILL BE OURS!"—refers to an electoral victory gained by rhetorical means, the work of orators and publicists, Sinclair himself included.

As a literary work and a historical document, then, *The Jungle* demands attention primarily as a flawed but strenuous effort to depict a kind of life that had found little previous expression in American writing. Sinclair had no tradition and few models to follow. Inspired by his recent knowledge of Socialism, his personal commitment to the movement, and his first-hand observations of working-class existence, he broke new literary ground. His tools of perception and expression were not always sharp, and at times he dug furiously rather than carefully, but in the end few readers—and not very many American writers—could ignore what he had done.

CHAPTER 4

The Peripatetic Radical

WHEN Doubleday, Page, and Company published *The Jungle* in February of 1906, the novel was an immediate, tumultuous, and international success. Favorable reviews came from figures as diverse as Winston Churchill and Bernard Shaw. In the legislative struggle for a Pure Food and Drug Act, President Roosevelt attracted further attention to *The Jungle* and its allegations about the meat packers. Long after 1906 the novel continued to impress readers throughout the world. Leon Harris has documented its influence even on the playwright Bertolt Brecht.[1] Jack London called it the *Uncle Tom's Cabin* of wage slavery. Literally overnight, Sinclair became famous, and the novel brought him wealth, initially earning him thirty thousand dollars.

His success launched him into a wide range of activities, most of which were directed at helping bring about the Socialist utopia described in the closing chapters of *The Jungle*. Many of his activities were shameless attempts to capitalize on his newly achieved reputation, and some were either motivated or damaged by the emotional shamble that his marriage had become, but all were connected with his progressive vision of the future. In 1927 he put his vision into the following words:

Scientific socialism is only a part of man's big job of understanding the blind forces of nature and subordinating them to his will. . . . We have partly suppressed the natural process of selection and elimination of the unfit; and we have either to go on and take rational control of the improvement of human stocks and the environment in which they grow, or else see our culture degenerate and perish. Birth control and eugenics are the merciful ways of eliminating the unfit; while sanitation and hygiene, the socialization of production and the abolition of parasitism, are the means of raising the new race.[2]

This statement, which may sound more coldly scientific than Sinclair intended, sheds some light on his seemingly eclectic activities and writings during the decade following *The Jungle,* up to America's involvement in World War I. Sinclair wrote eight novels, three books of nonfiction, a number of plays, and over a hundred articles and pamphlets on subjects ranging from war to communal living to venereal disease during these years. All were part of his quixotic crusade for a better world, less threatened by chance. It is difficult to sympathize with some of Sinclair's causes—like fasting or eugenics—and impossible to ignore the priggishness of many of his statements from 1906 to 1917 and afterwards. Yet it is important to examine his major expressions, not only for what they reveal about Upton Sinclair the person but also for their value as flawed but honorable attempts at exploring problems which other and better writers did not or would not touch.

I   The Industrial Republic

The Jungle released Sinclair's energies for numerous activities in 1906. He campaigned and lobbied for meat packing legislation, both encouraging and irritating President Roosevelt in the process.[3] He wrote several magazine articles about his novel, his vision of a better society, and his life;[4] he investigated working conditions in the glass-making and steel industries, and wrote muckraking articles which *Everybody's* magazine refused to publish after first indicating a strong interest in Sinclair's subjects.[5] He spent most of the thirty thousand dollars he earned from *The Jungle* on Helicon Hall, a highly publicized cooperative living experiment which ended in a disastrous fire in March 1907; and he wrote *The Industrial Republic,* a book explaining his personal Socialistic view of the future.[6]

Unlike most of Sinclair's early books, *The Industrial Republic* was never republished—not only because its original sales were small but also because Sinclair was embarrassed by certain rash predictions he made within its pages. Yet, it is a unique work which presents his overly hopeful case for an imminent Socialist state—the "Industrial Republic." Its expository prose is accompanied by charts, diagrams, photographs, and references to other writers. Outwardly, the book is only an argument for state Socialism; however, it is also a representation of the strong teleological spirit of pre-1917 Socialism in America, a paradigm of the radical search for benevolent historical order and predictability during the Progressive Era.

Sinclair's purpose in the book is to speculate what America will be like in ten years. His prognosis relies on "the method of evolution"— the continuing struggle for liberty in America, first in the eighteenth century, then from 1860 to 1865, and now in the twentieth century as the struggle has become one for industrial liberty. This struggle is not to be violent, however, for the Industrial Republic will come about "by a process as natural as inevitable as that by which a chick breaks out of its shell . . . at the proper hour" (ix). This process, Sinclair says, will be completed within one year of the 1912 Presidential election.

Sinclair's basic assumption is that capitalism, like the slave economy in the 1850's with which he continually draws parallels, has reached a breaking point. Sinclair expresses little regret over capitalism, since it is part of the grand evolutionary scheme. Industrial competition has "disciplined our laborers in diligence and skill, and our leaders in foresight, enterprise and administrative capacity," and it—especially through the creation of trusts—has "built us up a machine for the satisfying of all the material needs of civilization" (100-102). The present "social decay"—including alcoholism, slums, industrial accidents, and hopeless poverty—is evidence of the fact that industrial evolution is on the verge of a great leap forward.

This leap will follow a serious depression in 1908 or 1909. The depression will be the means of tutoring the American populace in advance of the 1912 elections, when ex-President Roosevelt will be the Republican candidate and William Randolph Hearst the Democratic one. Ironically, in view of later facts, Sinclair praises Hearst as an incipient Socialist, a traitor to his own class, and the man most likely to appeal to the oppressed masses during the depression. With the Socialist Party serving mainly to publicize and agitate, the people in 1912 will thus vote Hearst into office as another "Untried Hope," like Lincoln; and Hearst's latent Socialism will lead him to effect a transfer of power from capitalists to the people by nationalizing all major industries. Roosevelt, Sinclair says, is interested only in the rhetoric of reform.

The non-violent revolution managed by Hearst will usher in the Industrial Republic, a utopia involving little change in the outward appearances of industry but making tremendous internal differences. Workers will be compensated for the full value of their labor because profit will no longer be the motivating force of the economy. Poverty will thus disappear, as will its results—prostitution, war, drunkenness, crime. And best of all, the bourgeois spirit will no longer prevail in literature and honest writers will shape the public mind. In the last chapter of the book Sinclair describes his cooperative colony at Helicon Hall as a small example of what the future holds in store for mankind.

The Industrial Republic seems chiefly to continue the last chapter of *The Jungle*. Naive in political science and economics, it is a millenarian vision—deterministic, apocalyptic, with history culminating in one final and infinite moment. Sinclair's posture in the book is strangely theoretical, dogmatic, and anticipatory. Rather than the compassionate novelist of the first part of *The Jungle*, he is committed to dogma and vision rather than to any real compassion for the workers who suffer from the "social decay" of industrial evolution. *The Industrial Republic* documents his early response to the prophetic dreams and rhetoric of American Socialism. And its weaknesses suggest that as a writer Sinclair wrote best when he wrote as a sympathetic observer of real people and their problems.

II   *Rhetorical Excesses*

Helicon Hall, near Englewood Cliffs, New Jersey, was the achievement of a personal dream for Sinclair, the embodiment of cooperative ideals in the business of day to day living. During its short life from October 1906 to March 1907, it was a largely successful experiment in cooperative living and distribution involving Sinclair, his family, and nearly a hundred other persons. In 1920, looking back at his Helicon Hall experience, he said, "I have lived in the future; I have known those wider freedoms and opportunities that the future will grant to all men and women."[7] When fire destroyed the Hall, Sinclair was seriously affected by the loss. Frequent periods of estrangement from his wife, poor health, wandering between Socialist or single-tax communities, and occasional stays at a Michigan sanitarium run by J. H. Kellogg[8] formed the pattern of his life for several years afterwards. Not until his divorce from Meta Sinclair in 1912 and his remarriage shortly afterwards did he again experience long periods of emotional and marital stability.

From 1907 to 1912 Sinclair wrote much about his personal problems, including two books on the subject of achieving good health through diet and fasting. His significant productions during these years include two splenetic fictional attacks on capitalism: *The Metropolis* (1908) and *The Moneychangers* (1908). He also wrote a novel about idealism entitled *Samuel the Seeker* (1910), and *Love's Pilgrimage* (1911), the autobiographical account of his first marriage.

In *The Metropolis* Sinclair attempted to muckrake New York society. He was aided, he later said, by a woman informant, an unnameable lady "whose social position was impregnable" who provided him with scandalous facts concerning the lives of the leisurely rich in the city. Sinclair used Allan Montague, the son of the Allan Montague in *Manassas*, as his protagonist. Allan is a lawyer in search of a practice and moves easily through high urban society. When the novel opens in a contemporary setting of lavish apartments, spectacular country estates, and irresponsibly driven automobiles, Allan has just come to the city to establish his legal career. His younger brother Oliver, who has been around long enough to make influential friends and sponge parasitically off the rich, introduces him to several wealthy families. Within a few months Allan sees all he wants of reckless consuming, high-class immorality (one rich lady tries unsuccessfully to seduce him), and business corruption. In his last words in the story, aimed at little brother Oliver, Allan says he will give up his connections with the wealthy, move to a simple apartment, and "find out if there isn't some way in New York for a man to earn an honest living."[9]

Even Sinclair later admitted that *The Metropolis* was "a poor book."[10] Resembling Veblen in its exposure of conspicuous consumption among the leisure class, it suggests that Sinclair wanted to believe in reformation of the rich rather than revolt against them; but it finishes as a self-righteous yet vaguely envious exaggeration of society. Through Allan Montague Sinclair criticizes low-cut gowns, extravagant meals, interest in mysticism, homosexuality, dilettantism in general, and the reading of Baudelaire and Wilde. Potential good qualities of the novel—the absence of Socialist propaganda and the needed indictment of gaudiness and waste among a real and highly visible leisure class in 1908—are seriously compromised by overt moralizing and by Sinclair's tenuous attempt to prove that leisure-class males waste time sullying themselves in New York's Tenderloin district. The novel seems mostly to reflect the bias against the city that Sinclair developed as an awed and frightened child.

The Moneychangers, written during and after the unfavorable reception of *The Metropolis*, exhibits more authorial control but is flawed by an artificial plot. The story also involves Allan Montague, but concentrates on Dan Waterman, elderly head of the Steel Trust, who resembles J. P. Morgan. Waterman attempts to rape Lucy Dupree, an old friend of Allan's, is foiled by Allan himself, and then learns that Lucy is in love with one of Waterman's capitalist rivals,

Stanley Ryder. To gain revenge, Waterman destroys Ryder financially by luring him into extravagant business deals and then creating
a panic on Wall Street. Finally, when the panic seems to get out of
hand, the government steps in and allows Waterman to end it by
taking open control over a steel company that he had been
manipulating covertly. At the end of the novel both Lucy and Stanley
Ryder commit suicide. The whole sordid mess encourages Allan
Montague to state, "I am going into politics. I am going to try to teach
the people."[11]

   The Moneychangers is certainly not great fiction, but it is ingenious
in suggesting sexual motives for the financial manipulations of the
villainous Waterman-Morgan. As an implied portrait of Morgan, of
course, the novel is overdone, inaccurate, and possibly libelous. In its
veiled retelling of the controversial purchase of Tennessee Coal and
Iron by U. S. Steel in 1907, as well as the panic of that year, and in its
surprising lack of invective against rich men as individuals—except
for Dan Waterman—*The Moneychangers* is a noticeable improvement over *A Captain of Industry*, Sinclair's earlier attempt to exploit
similar material. It demonstrates to some small extent Sinclair's
ability to create novels out of recent events, an ability which he was to
use to far better effect later in *Oil!, Boston,* and *Co-Op.* Unfortunately, Sinclair was completely unable or unwilling to deal with a less
fantastic but more empathetic Socialist proletariat in either *The
Metropolis* or *The Moneychangers*.

III   *Sinclair the Seeker*

   After he finished The *Moneychangers* Sinclair may have been
tempted to follow Allan Montague into his attempt to "teach the
people" through politics, but he wisely decided that two novels with
the same central and overly genteel consciousness were enough.
Besides, he was temporarily drawn away from fiction by an increasing
interest in the problems of health. One result of this interest was a
book, *Good Health and How We Won It* (1909), written with Michael
Williams, telling of his various diets and eating practices. Later he
wrote articles on numerous aspects of health for Bernarr McFadden's
Physical Culture magazine and compiled *The Fasting Cure* (1911), a
book presenting evidence, by Sinclair and others, that fasting is an
effective cure for many ailments. Such works are part of an
undercurrent of bizarre interests (including various kinds of psychic
phemonena) that have little obvious relationship to Sinclair's political
and social views but which occupied much of his time for several

decades. This "spookology," a term used by some of Sinclair's friends to describe such interests,[12] reveals the breadth of the author's concerns and sheds some interesting light on his personality; but it includes little worthwhile writing and deserves little attention in this study.

Two novels from the end of Sinclair's period of personal frustration, however, do deserve attention. *Samuel the Seeker* (1910) marks Sinclair's return to political considerations, and *Love's Pilgrimage* (1911) his attempt to objectify, through autobiographical fiction, what had happened to his marriage and to his strong early dream "of a noble and beautiful love."

Sinclair wrote *Samuel the Seeker* in 1909 amid a flurry of other activities. After finishing *The Moneychangers* in the summer of 1908, he spent several months crossing the nation from east to west, stopping when possible to visit reformers (like Judge Ben Lindsey in Denver) and writers (like the poet George Sterling in Carmel, California) who were sympathetic to Socialism. He spent the winter of 1908–9 in Carmel, where he founded a dramatic group to present several one act plays that he had written. These plays, along with a dramatization of *The Jungle*, were never very popular, but they were useful literary and political activities.[13] In a dramatization of *Prince Hagen*, for instance, Sinclair changed his pre-Socialist plot by having legislators expropriate Hagen's illegal wealth.[14] In "The Second-Story Man" he wrote a moderately perceptive play dealing with the social and economic factors behind a burglar's life of crime.[15] After his efforts in theater, Sinclair turned to writing a novel about a young religious seeker who eventually discovers that Socialism is the only true faith.

Lacking subtlety in plot and characterization, and intended as something "elemental and naive,"[16] *Samuel the Seeker* nevertheless identifies opposing social philosophies in America before World War I and reveals the nation's reactionary willingness to suppress the right of free speech when it is exercised by the political left. In the parabolic story Samuel Prescott is a member of the "Seekers," a fictitious religious group "who had broken with the churches because they would not believe what was taught—holding that it was every man's duty to read the Word of God for himself and to follow where it led him."[17] Accordingly, he sets out on his own at seventeen. He first falls under the influence of a college professor, probably William Graham Sumner, who teaches Social Darwinism, proclaiming that the advance of the race demands the sacrifice of the unfit. After he unsuccessfully tries to sacrifice himself, believing that he is poor and unfit, Samuel takes up an opposing posture—that the poor and oppressed must not sacrifice themselves but must instead fight violently for survival. Following this philosophy, Samuel burglarizes the home of a rich clergyman. Then, reformed by the young daughter of the minister, he adopts altruism as his personal creed. He now finds himself in agreement with the Socialists, especially since no one else seems interested in eliminating corruption and inequality. Finally, Samuel attends a Socialist rally which is violently disrupted by the police. At the close of the novel he lies on the ground unconscious and bleeding, the victim of police brutality. Along with *Jimmie Higgins* (1919), *100%* (1920), and *They Call Me Carpenter* (1922), *Samuel the Seeker* is a sharp attack on middle-class political reactionaries.

Love's Pilgrimage is a far different kind of novel. When it was written Sinclair knew that his marriage was breaking up as he and Meta could not resolve their difficulties. He realized that his own interests would be best served by a divorce, but he found the idea of divorce difficult to accept emotionally. His novel, then, was an effort to cope with this situation. Although Sinclair presented it as fiction, and changed the names of Meta and himself to the generic "Corydon" and "Thyrsis" (the two shepherds in Milton's "L'Allegro"), *Love's Pilgrimage* is more autobiographical than fictitious.

The book is not a satisfying work unless the reader brings to it some interest in or knowledge of Upton Sinclair. But given this prerequisite, it is a remarkably candid document which criticizes aspects of Sinclair's own personality, makes a feminist plea for the personal and intellectual needs of married women, and—almost as an afterthought—implies that divorce is sometimes justified. It is difficult to ascertain whether this account conforms to Sinclair's intentions, or if he had others in mind. In his autobiography he claims that he wrote much of the story as Meta wanted it told; but he also says that he intended to write a novel about a "modern marriage" in which a man and a wife could agree to separate and still remain friends.[18] It is also possible that Sinclair was quite interested in explaining how marriage tended to restrict his energies as an artist-genius and offered his wife no offsetting advantages. Guilt, conscious or unconscious, may well have been one of the motivating factors behind the book. For almost a decade, since his marriage in 1900, Sinclair had made extraordinary demands on his wife, insisting that they live in poverty so that he could write, and generally subordinating her needs and desires to the necessities of his career. Although he knew that Meta was constitutionally prone to depression, indecision, and ailments that may have been psychosomatic in origin, he certainly could not have believed that she was entirely to blame for her unhappiness.

The plot of this extremely long book (over six hundred fifty pages) follows the outlines of Sinclair's life from 1900 to 1905, with some significant glances into childhood and adolescence. The story is interrupted between each of its twenty-six sections by dialogue between "Thyrsis" (Sinclair) and "Corydon" (Meta) who, from a current (1910) vantage point, comment briefly on their story as it is related by an omniscient narrator. The plot itself concerns the attempts of Thyrsis to fulfill his potential as a poet after he falls in love with and marries Corydon. Thyrsis faces the same oppressive situation—an inexorable desire to create combined with an inability to sell his work—that Sinclair did. Like Sinclair, he eventually becomes a Socialist and thinks that most of his troubles are economic in origin, the result of a capitalistic literary market. However, throughout his literary trials his energies are compromised by his duties as a husband and father, and by the emotional problems experienced by Corydon. Generally in agreement intellectually with her husband's argument that his first duty is to his genius, Corydon is nevertheless driven to depression, sickness, attempted suicide, and near-adultery by the poverty in which she must live and by the emotional tensions in her marriage.

Although the novel presents an ideological argument asserting that the institution of marriage is often a constraining economic arrangement, the real interest in the story is the clash of personalities. Influenced by a puritanical divinity student who obviously represents Sinclair's friend, Reverend Moir, Thyrsis is an extreme religious moralist who has eschewed religious dogma and is now almost neurotically insistent on expressing his genius. In marriage, particularly in sexual relations, he suffers from an agonizing tension between his strong sexual desires and his equally strong sexual fears. The fears are motivated by his religious upbringing, by his desperate earnestness to avoid a second child, and by a possible unconscious fear of castration. For example, at one point the "sex factor" in Thyrsis's life is described as "some bird of prey that circled in the sky just above him—its shadow filling him with a continual fear."[19] In this respect *Love's Pilgrimage* is an exposé, with perhaps some contritional exaggeration, of disturbing tendencies in Sinclair's own personality.

Corydon is a more empathetic character, the most realistic portrayal in all of Sinclair's novels. The basis of her personality is an understandable need for love and affection. Her response to sexual relations is therefore quite different from Thyrsis's. "She was like a little child about it, so free, so spontaneous, so genuine; Thyrsis marvelled at her utter naturalness" (202). She is initially devoted to her husband and his literary dreams, struggling to be the kind of wife he thinks he should have, until she is psychologically unable to continue in such a role. In *Love's Pilgrimage* Sinclair candidly depicts the clash between Thyrsis and Corydon without implying that the failure of the marriage is mostly the fault of the wife. He does try to show that marriage is often an economic institution, but this kind of Socialist argument is only partly convincing. The real villain is the bondage of love itself when it is institutionalized in marriage. Traditional marriages, Sinclair suggests, tend to prevent the personal fulfillment of women as well as men. In the section titles of the novel, Thyrsis is "The Victim," love is "The Snare," sexual intercourse is "The Bait," and married life is "The Capture" or "The Treadmill." Thyrsis loves Corydon but hates the situation that love sanctions.

Although the novel abounds with flights of purpling rhetoric whenever Sinclair describes the emotions of Thyrsis, *Love's Pilgrimage* is honest and effective fiction. Largely unstructured save by chronology and psychological tensions, and arriving at no definite resolution, its formlessness works well as a depiction of uncertainty in the relations of its two characters. Another fine aspect of the book is the objective, if not confessional, manner in which Sinclair portrays Thyrsis's limitations. *Love's Pilgrimage* is also an important work because Sinclair boldly depicts human sexuality, describes childbirth, and strongly suggests a need for public knowledge of birth control methods.[20] His frank discussion of these issues, accepted casually today, was sensational in 1911.

IV *Sex, Disease, and Socialism*

In Sinclair's career *Love's Pilgrimage* was a necessary book, partly an act of contrition and apology, and a means of easing the emotional tension within him at the end of his first marriage in order that he might move forward in his role as a social critic and radical propagandist. It is unfortunate that he never returned to this mode of autobiographical yet detached fiction. Perhaps it was a completely unique effort, a "sport" in his career prompted by his conflicting feelings toward Meta at the time. In any event, he moved on to another stage of his career, ironically contradicting his arguments against marriage in *Love's Pilgrimage*. In 1911, when Meta finally ran off with one of Sinclair's friends and Sinclair himself fell in love with Mary Craig Kimbrough, a proper young Southern woman who had made friends with literary and political radicals in New York, Sinclair sued for divorce. But the suit was refused in New York courts, and he therefore left for Europe, where through his friendship with the Dutch poet Frederick van Eeden he arranged for a divorce in Holland. The divorce was granted and in the spring of 1913 he married Mary Craig Kimbrough at her family home in Virginia. It was the beginning of a long and successful marriage in which Sinclair's new wife gave moral support to his radical activities, successfully managed his financial affairs, and collaborated with him on several literary ventures during the following four decades.

The first collaboration began before their wedding. Sinclair's interest in health problems led him naturally to the subject of venereal disease, where it joined with his moralistic ideas about sex and with his economic determinism. He was profoundly influenced by Eugene Brieux's play *Damaged Goods (Les Avaries)* showing the results of untreated syphilis and pleading for public education.[21] In 1913 he even turned Brieux's play into a novel bearing the same title. Interested in creating his own plot and in attributing the prevalence of venereal disease partly to capitalism, Sinclair began writing two novels in 1912 which show the unfortunate consequences of gonorrhea in the life of a young Southern woman. It may be important that at this time Sinclair saw a need for Socialism to counteract the prevalence of venereal disease, whereas other radicals were more concerned, in 1913 at least, with politics and labor, particularly the garment workers' strike in Paterson, New Jersey.

Although *Sylvia* (1913) and *Sylvia's Marriage* (1914) were published separately a year apart, they can be discussed as one story inspired largely by the author's new wife. *Sylvia* begins detailing the life of Sylvia Castleman, a beautiful and sensitive Virginia belle who is sent north to finishing school. Sylvia's story is narrated by her long-time friend, Mary Abbott, a forty year old woman who has become a Socialist. Mary Abbott explains that when Sylvia was a young marriageable woman she caused all men who knew her to fall in love with her. Frank Shirley is one of these men and remains in

Sylvia's good graces until he is arrested in a house of prostitution near Harvard College. Unable to marry the stigmatized Frank Shirley, she becomes engaged to Douglas Van Tuiver, the scion of a wealthy New England family. Sylvia's uncertainty about her feelings for Van Tuiver is further complicated by a friend's warning that Van Tuiver may have venereal disease. Persuaded, however, by her family's need for money and by Van Tuiver's assurance that he could not have contracted a disease, she marries him. At the end of the novel Sinclair suggests that the marriage may not be a happy one and that there is more to Sylvia's story.

Sylvia's Marriage begins after the marriage, when Mary Abbott becomes Sylvia's close friend and introduces her to social reform and to the need for Socialism. These lessons are soon reinforced by events in Sylvia's life. Her child is born blind, the result of gonorrhea and the failure of doctors to recognize the symptoms at birth. Sylvia then learns that her husband had lied to her, and had in fact engaged in an infectious sexual affair. Sylvia leaves him and returns to her Virginia home, where she scandalizes her family by openly campaigning against venereal disease and by demanding that her sister's fiancé present a medical certificate guaranteeing that he is free of infection. Finally, Frank Shirley returns. Sylvia has learned that the story of his escapade in the Cambridge brothel was a misrepresentation of the truth—he is in fact morally and bodily clean—but when the novel ends she has not decided to marry him.

The Sylvia books are only adequate fictional achievements. When they were published, they were highly needed presentations of a serious and seldom discussed social problem—today they testify to the broad range of Sinclair's social conscience. But as fiction, even as muckraking novels, they are somewhat unnecessarily burdened with Socialistic doctrine, with characters who often seem to be two-dimensional cutouts for the sake of propaganda or melodrama, and with some identifiable priggishness behind a rational concern for public health. A good example of this last trait occurs in *Sylvia* when the heroine says to Frank Shirley, whom she loves, "Frank, I don't want you to kiss me any more until we're married. I'm going to stop doing everything that makes me ashamed."[22] Mary Abbott expresses a more subtle prudery when she tells Sylvia that "There is very little sex-life for women without a money-price made clear in advance,"[23] thereby articulating Sinclair's belief that marriage, like prostitution, is often a woman's way of earning economic rewards. Ironically, at another point in the story Sinclair has Mary state her dislike for "prudery and purity and chivalry."

Particularly disturbing in the novels is the combination of extreme rationality in matters of sex and love and the subjectivity, idealism, and sentimentality that pervades Sinclair's diction. For example, early in *Sylvia*, Mary Abbott describes Sylvia in "the glow of her youth" as "eager, impetuous, swept with gusts of merriment and tenderness, like a mountain lake in April"(19). It is difficult at times to understand how the Socialist narrator, who has worked as a child labor investigator in heavy industries, could speak as rapturously and continually about the aristocratic Sylvia as she does. Like other Sinclair works, *Sylvia* and *Sylvia's Marriage* suggest a latent admiration—some might say envy—of right-hearted aristocrats. In this case the aristocrats happen to be Southerners, and Sinclair's sympathetic presentation of them contrasts noticeably with his harsh treatment of the South in *Manassas*. *Sylvia* is dedicated "To the People at Home," obliquely indicating Sinclair's newfound willingness to accept his Southern roots.

The sentimental treatment of Sylvia Castleman obscures the potential of developing the intriguing narrator, Mary Abbott, into an effective character. Mary, who is interested in Christian Science, fasting, Theosophy, New Thought, and Socialism, obviously represents Sinclair yet is sketchily portrayed and interesting primarily for her role in the unusual proletarian-aristocrat friendship in the story. Sinclair obviously intended his readers to pay attention only to Sylvia's encounters with venereal disease, wealth, and the kind of male chauvinism which motivates one doctor to tell her that she has no right to hate her husband for giving her a blind child because gonorrhea is a common infection among even the finest men.

V *Fantasy and Utopia*

Sinclair's next significant literary venture after the Sylvia story was *The Millennium*, a novel serialized in the *Appeal to Reason* in 1914 but not published in book form until 1924. A fantasy rather than a novel of prediction, *The Millennium* oddly cuts against the grain of any faith in revolutionary politics by emphasizing cooperative alternatives to capitalism rather than reform or revolution itself.

The story tells of a millennium reached in stages. When the world is destroyed by radioactive gas (an interesting idea prior to 1945!), eleven persons escape by airplane and return to the ground when the danger from the gas is past. The eleven persons are representative of various social classes and viewpoints; the main character is Billy Kingdon, a Socialist. At first they develop a capitalistic society motivated by a desire to possess food tablets (wealth) invented and exploited by an ex-butler. When this situation becomes unbearable, a revolution of sorts is staged by an ex-minister and the wife of an ex-plutocrat, who plot a strike. The strike, however, fails. Finally, the discontents achieve the cooperative commonwealth only by migrating to the bucolic setting of the Pocantico Hills, where they are instructed by Billy Kingdon.[24]

There are ironies in the fantasy of *The Millennium*. First, the millennium can be achieved only when a catastrophic accident forces (which is represented by the pill-manufacturing ex-butler). Second, the intellectual class, represented by a fellow named Granville, conspires with the proletariat for entirely selfish reasons. Finally, the millennium can be achieved only when a catastrophe accident forces persons of good will to escape from a capitalistic society. Sinclair's Socialism in this story is neither reformist nor revolutionary. It is escapist. Apparently, Sinclair meant to suggest that small Socialist islands could be established by those who could no longer stomach life under capitalism.

While refusing to offer much hope for reform or revolution, *The Millennium* expresses a utopian hope that Sinclair had long cherished. Since adolescence he had struggled to remain free from the clutches of materialism and greed. This kind of idealism inspired his first novel, *Springtime and Harvest*, made his Helicon Hall experiment seem possible, and made him appealing to California voters later during the depression. In this sense, then, *The Millennium* was a regressive novel, a falling back to an earlier position, as it was also regressive in its use of fantasy, which Sinclair had not exploited extensively since *Prince Hagen* and *The Overman* in 1902 and 1903.

Both *The Millennium* and the Sylvia novels are obvious clues to Sinclair's departure from the mainstream of American radicalism. Most Socialists, Anarchists, Bohemians, and social critics of other persuasions were drawn to New York City and to *The Masses*, the vibrant radical magazine, in the years preceding and during World War I. Sinclair, while contributing occasional pieces to *The Masses* and developing a friendship with Floyd Dell, a prominent Bohemian and Socialist, began to look southward and westward after 1913. He grew close to his new wife's family, even living at the ancestral home in Mississippi for a while in 1914 and 1915. In these years he also became concerned about labor problems in Western mines, the subject of *King Coal*. His sense of audience also shifted geographically. Rather than appeal to the urbanity and sophistication of New York radicals, whose liberal attitudes toward sexual behavior and liquor repelled him, he found a more congenial audience in Westerners: Populists and ex-Populists, the kind of people who read the *Appeal to Reason* and felt a need for someone like Sinclair to teach them about life and society. Although such expectations of his audience often tended to bring out the didactic and banal in Sinclair, as was partly the case in *The Millennium*, it sometimes encouraged him to a performance similar to *The Jungle*. In 1917 *King Coal* was such a performance.

CHAPTER 5

The Muckraker as Novelist: King Coal

*K*ING *Coal* is a case study in the techniques Sinclair used best as a novelist. In,writing it he collected objective information about labor difficulties in the mines of Colorado, accepted literary assistance from both his editor and his wife, and remained firm in his intention of supporting coal workers through both publicity and art. The result was a novel with both factual and rhetorical merits, not as powerful as *The Jungle* nor with much autobiographical or psychological content, but a readable and only partly sentimental work that effectively pointed its reader's attention to a serious industrial problem. At the time of publication in 1917 the interest of readers was unfortunately aborted by American entrance into World War I, and the novel was something of a failure commercially. Yet as a significant step in Sinclair's career, a not entirely anticipated exercise in fiction rather than propaganda, and as a sign of rekindled concern for industrial justice, *King Coal* is one of Sinclair's novels still worth an extended discussion.

I *Putting the Clothes on the Story*

Although *King Coal* was published in the fall of 1917, Sinclair's involvement with his subject began four years earlier. In September 1913, and immediately before he began to write *Sylvia's Marriage*, he began to learn of unsuccessful efforts by the United Mine Workers and the Western Federation of Miners to establish their unions in the Colorado coal fields. At that time, sixty years before officials of the Teamsters Union found themselves chauffered to Washington in the Presidential jet, the issue of unionization was in violent dispute. Many industrialists hoped for the continuation of the open shop, and their management often worked to exclude unions altogether from their industries. Nowhere was this more the case than in Rocky Mountain coal camps, where fuel companies owned not only the mines but also the houses where the workers lived, the stores where

80

they shopped, the public buildings where they voted and their children attended school, and in some cases even the landscape. Such conditions made it easy for management to identify and exclude union organizers, and sometimes even to fire union members, as well as to control local politics and therefore prevent pro-union reform efforts.

In late 1913 the United Mine Workers, who had been organizing both openly and, where necessary, covertly, responded to anti-union prejudice by calling a number of strikes in the Colorado fields. The strikes were eventually broken by the power of the coal companies, particularly the Colorado Fuel and Iron Company, in conjunction with the use of state militia. But the accompanying violence rose to civil war proportions and set the stage for an eventual tolerance of unions in the coal industry after investigations by a congressional committee and the Industrial Relations Commission. The point of greatest violence occurred in April of 1914 when followers of the situation were shocked to learn that in Ludlow, Colorado, troops had opened fire on a tent camp of strikers and their families. Eleven women and two children were killed.

In late 1913 and early 1914 Sinclair was busy on his manuscript of *Sylvia's Marriage* as he and his new wife traveled from Europe, where they had spent a honeymoon summer, to New York City for a short while, and then to Bermuda for the remainder of the winter. Amid this movement and in spite of his great interest in the problem of venereal disease, Sinclair maintained—or regained—his concern for industrial justice. In January 1914 he published in several Socialist papers an open letter to Vincent Astor, requesting Astor to aid the dispossessed with his family wealth and to support Socialism.[1] Remarkably, Astor replied to Sinclair in an open letter of his own in which he expressed an awareness of social and industrial problems, stated a belief that such evils could be eliminated "without overturning the fundamental basis upon which our Government and social fabric is founded," and drew Sinclair's attention to his personal contact with leaders of the American Federation of Labor (A.F. of L.), "whom the great mass of the working people of our country have authorized to speak for them," who had convinced him that the conditions of workers were steadily improving.[2] Sinclair's personal reply to Astor's letter expresses a compassionate understanding of working conditions in industrial America.

Dated January 19, 1914, Sinclair's twelve page statement begins with a grateful acknowledgment of Astor's willingness to state his views. The letter then goes on to point out that Astor's opinions have been shaped by the leaders of the labor movement, who tend to become middle-class bureaucrats, and not by any real contact with "the life and death of millions of our suffering fellow-mortals." The A. F. of L., Sinclair says, represents only a small minority of workers (and even among them, there is considerable support for Socialism), none of whom are unskilled. The conditions of the unskilled worker, who has seen living costs rise forty per cent in ten years, is tragic and will only be remedied through "the abolishment of private property in the instruments and means of production of the necessities of life," which Sinclair felt could be accomplished through a constitutional amendment similar to the one that abolished private property in human beings.[3]

The general subject of this unique Sinclair-Astor correspondence became specific and emphatic after the Ludlow Massacre in April. By then Sinclair and his wife had settled in New York City where they were eagerly available to hear the details of the massacre from the wife of the president of the Western Federation of Miners. Learning that the Colorado Fuel and Iron Company was a Rockefeller concern, Sinclair tried unsuccessfully to interview John D. Rockefeller, Jr. and then organized a demonstration in front of the Standard Oil Building—an activity that, incidentally, put the writer in jail for two days.[4] Afterwards, with his wife continuing an orderly demonstration, he traveled to Colorado to personally investigate the coal industry.

What he learned in Colorado is suggested in a letter, apparently unanswered, that he wrote to Rockefeller from Denver on May 26. Urging Rockefeller "to hear . . . the pleading of the social conscience," Sinclair hoped to convince him to use his power and wealth to improve working conditions in mines. Sinclair's letter began with this statement:

About a month ago I addressed a letter to you on the subject of the Colorado strike; I called at your office with the wife of one of the representatives of the miners, but without being permitted to see you. At that time I had only hearsay evidence concerning the situation; but now I have been upon the scene, and have talked with scores of victims of the crimes that have been committed. I have met a mother who was made a target for militia bullets while she dragged her two children away from the blazing village of Ludlow; another whose three children were left behind to perish in that inferno. It seems to me as if the air I breathed were full of the smoke of powder and the scent of burning human flesh; as if my ears were deafened with the screams of women and children.[5]

Like his earlier experience in Packingtown, Sinclair's Colorado trip brought him into direct contact with the working class, affected him emotionally, and provided the basis for a more realistic fiction than he had been able to produce through secondhand knowledge in such novels as *The Metropolis* and *Sylvia*.

Upon returning from Colorado, Sinclair did not immediately begin his new novel. Since *Sylvia* and *Sylvia's Marriage* had not been financial successes, the Sinclairs were low on money. Sinclair therefore proposed to compile and edit an anthology of social protest literature, *The Cry for Justice*, for the John C. Winston Company. Winston advanced a thousand dollars, which enabled Sinclair to spend the rest of 1914 and the early part of 1915 collecting material for his six hundred page anthology which when finished brought together a wide variety of selections from classical humanists and from contemporary writers concerned with social problems.[6] Complete with an introduction by Jack London (to whom Sinclair turned after Theodore Roosevelt declined to introduce the book), *The Cry for Justice* was, as James Gilbert has pointed out in his study of modern literary radicalism in America, the "last, most comprehensive statement of the older, eclectic attitude towards Socialist art."[7]

Finally, in the summer of 1915 Sinclair was able to begin a novel dealing with industrial strife in Colorado. His title was *King Coal*, and he worked on his manuscript for nearly a year. Throughout this time he remained excited about the events that had led up to the Ludlow Massacre. In May 1915 he even composed an open letter to Rockefeller and sent it for approval to over two hundred and fifty American liberals; in it he wrote, "We hold you, John D. Rockefeller, Jr., guilty of murder in the first degree, and we here indict you before the bar of humanity."[8]

In the opinion of Sinclair's editor, however, such emotional involvement did not result in a good novel. When Sinclair sent the first section of his story to George P. Brett, editor and president of the Macmillan Company, Brett courteously expressed reservations, saying, "I wish that you could take more time to the story and give it, by close revision and rewriting where necessary, that flavor of good literature which it now, by reason of haste, sometimes lacks and which you are so well qualified to give it."[9] Sinclair either did not heed Brett's advice or had different notions about "good literature," for when he sent his entire manuscript to Macmillan in May 1916, he received the following comments from Brett:

I hɾ   ɪte greatly to advise you to revise or rewrite "King Coal" because I recogɪ ze the fact that the book is salable as it is and that it will, at any rate to a considerable extent, create the impression which you wish to make.

At the same time "King Coal" is a great disappointment to me. You have here, as I said before, a great opportunity and the chance of making a work of art which will live for all time. The manuscript as I see it now will not in my opinion live beyond its first furor or sale, and it is not, I am sorry to say, in my opinion, a work of art at all in its present shape.

Moreover, I suspect the kind of rewriting that this book needs would be more than you would care to undertake, and perhaps more than it is really worth while to undertake because to do what I think should be done with the book would require the forgetting during the rewriting of the book, the Colorado field altogether and many of its incidents.

Coal is one of the great facts of the world and "King Coal," as this novel should be called, would, if rewritten along the lines that I think would make it a worthwhile work of art, require that it should be a novel of the coal world for the world and not merely for the Colorado strike.

Again, the latter part of the MS as it now is, is not a novel at all, it is merely a string of facts from the Colorado strike put into the mouths or action of a few fictitious characters. [10]

Brett's comments suggest that he wanted a story of coal on the scale of Norris's work on wheat. But Sinclair, by nature and conviction a reformer, and in addition to that a Socialist, could not produce a folk-novel like *The Octopus*.

For some reason which is not entirely clear, Sinclair nevertheless accepted Brett's argument. Rather than seek publication elsewhere he allowed his wife to write Brett and suggest that she could help him revise the manuscript. It may well be that at the time Sinclair was suffering from an adverse public image as a "crank" interested primarily in fasting, diet reform, and venereal disease—and therefore wished to produce a reputable work of art supported by a reputable publisher.

In writing to Brett, Mary Craig Sinclair was convinced that her husband "was not much of a psychologist. He thought of characters in a book merely as vehicles for carrying his ideas." [11] Brett agreed to read the manuscript again after the revision, which involved the fleshing out of characters in the story, especially one Irish girl, Mary Burke, the daughter of a miner, who had not even been described in the first version. Mary Craig and Upton thus called their revising "putting the clothes on Mary Burke."[12]

The Sinclairs completed their work on the manuscript a year later, and Brett then agreed to publish the novel. The long period of gestation, during which Sinclair absorbed information and grew emotionally attached to the cause of the miners, and the equally long period of composition both helped and harmed the final product. *King Coal,* when it was finally published in September 1917, was certainly a more objective novel than it would have been in 1915. However, by 1917 America's involvement in World War I had siphoned off the interest that Sinclair hoped would make his book a popular success. The problem of coal workers was simply not a strong competitor for public attention in the midst of the German submarine threat, the preparedness controversy, and, finally, war. Most likely, a powerful, direct plea for understanding in Colorado, even if it lacked the kind of propaganda-free art that George Brett demanded, would have accomplished Sinclair's own purposes better than his eventual attempt to make art out of muckraking. However, the writing of *King Coal* was a significant learning experience which prepared the way for the recognized achievements of *Oil!* and *Boston* in the following decade.

II *Labor and Love*

The plot of *King Coal* makes no attempt to directly follow the Colorado strife of 1913 and 1914; rather, it follows the attempt of an affluent young college student, Hal Warner, to personally investigate working conditions in the coal mining camps of a mountainous area which, though unidentified in the novel, is obviously Colorado. Hal Warner is himself the son of a coal magnate, but this fact is concealed from the reader until the last part of the story. From the start Sinclair depicts Hal as a twenty year old seeker of "experience" who for one summer steps outside his social class in order to verify or reject the conflicting economic facts that he has learned in three years of college courses and in the writings of muckrakers. The coal camp where he finds his answers by passing as a worker is not one owned by his family; instead, it is the North Valley camp of the General Fuel Company (G.F.C.), owned by Peter Harrigan, benefactor of Hal's college and most powerful of American coal lords. Although Sinclair uses Hal Warner's movements and thoughts to present a panorama of working conditions and politics in the coal camps, Hal's own personality and the conflicts within it are an integral part of the story.

The novel is divided into four books. In Book One, "The Domain of King Coal," Hal observes working and living conditions in North Valley. When he first tries to enter the camp he is suspected of being a labor agitator and is chased away. But posing as "Joe Smith," he eventually gets a job at the mine and begins to associate with a wide variety of ethnic groups and nationalities hired by the G.F.C. As he does in *The Jungle*, Sinclair stresses this ethnic diversity: "The Americans and English and Scotch looked down upon the Welsh and the Irish; the Welsh and the Irish looked down upon the Dagoes and Frenchies; the Dagoes and Frenchies looked down upon Polacks and Hunkies, those in turn upon Greeks, Bulgarians and 'Monty-negroes', and so on through a score of races of Eastern Europe, Lithuanians, Slovaks, and Croatians, Armenians, Roumanians, Rumelians, Ruthenians—ending up with Greasers, niggers, and last and lowest, Japs."[13] As a worker in the polyglot community, Hal discovers that the management denies its employees two important legal rights: the right to organize into a union and the right to have a check-weighman, paid by workers themselves, to insure accurate weighing of each miner's coal production. When he meets a United Mine Workers organizer who is operating clandestinely in the camp, Hal is somewhat uncertain about unionization because it has previously been linked in his mind with industrial violence; but he sees clearly the need to keep the company from cheating the miners and decides to begin a campaign for a check-weighman. As he becomes involved in these affairs Hal meets a bitter young Irish woman, Mary Burke, who recognizes his upper-class origins, interprets his friendliness as romantic interest, and begs him to take her away from the mines. Hal replies, "I'm not free. There is someone else" (75).

In Book Two, "The Serfs of King Coal," Hal is rudely introduced to industrial injustice. The management, which controls every aspect of life in the mining camp, opposes the election of the check-weighman, who is Hal himself, and throws Hal in the company jail on a spurious charge of accepting a bribe. In jail Hal discovers that his thoughts were "no longer troubled with fears of labour union domination and walking delegate tyranny; on the contrary, he became suddenly willing for the people of North Valley to have a union, and to be as tyrannical as they knew how"(143). When Hal convinces his jailers that he has outside connections, they decide to release him; he, in turn, assumes that he will go home "counting his education complete"(150). But his plans are disrupted by a tragic explosion in the mine and by his realization that the company is more interested in saving coal than saving lives when rescue efforts proceed without haste. He decides, therefore, to do what he can to publicize the company's negligence. Meanwhile Mary Burke pleads once more with him to take her away; this time she says that she finds it hard to believe in the "other girl." Hal responds by saying that if he took Mary away and accepted the "anything" that she would do for him in return, it would weaken his own character.

Hal leaves the camp in the third section of the novel, "The Henchmen of King Coal," and tries to convince officials in a nearby town that criminal charges should be pressed against the G.F.C. But the only person who will listen to him is a correspondent for a "yellow" newspaper. Everyone else appears to be owned by the coal company. Finally, when Hal learns that Percy Harrigan, the son of "King Coal" himself, is passing through town in his private train, he confronts Percy with details of the tragedy at the mine. Coincidentally, Percy Harrigan is a classmate of Hal's; in a further and weakening coincidence, Hal's fiancée, Jessie Arthur, happens to be in Percy's party. Although young Harrigan is reluctant to do anything, Hal's efforts finally result in increased rescue efforts at the mine, where many workers are now dead. Hal takes his fiancée to the camp, where she is of course sympathetic to the workers' plight; but being a leisure-class woman, she cannot fully appreciate Hal's concern. When Hal kisses Jessie good-bye at the end of Book Three, he is torn emotionally between his love for her and his social conscience.

In the last book of the novel, "The Will of King Coal," the miners organize a strike. In this effort both Hal and Mary Burke are leaders. The strikers demand no wage increases; what they want are a recognition of their rights to a union and to a check-weighman, an assurance from the company that the mines will be made safer from explosions, and the right to trade at other than company stores. Despite these mild demands the strike fails because the United Mine Workers cannot support it; Hal learns from a U.M.W. official that the workers must first achieve a large union membership. Hal agrees, and he convinces the miners to call off the impromptu strike and build up the membership of the U.M.W. He then has a last long conversation with Mary Burke, who tells him candidly that in spite of his idealism and conscience he has not completely escaped the mentality of the upper class, and this limitation, she says, is why he will not let himself love her. Hal finally leaves North Valley in the company of his conservative older brother. He intends to finish

college. His plans after that, as he tells Mary, are "to fight for the
working people. When the big strike comes, as we know it's coming
in this coal-country, I'll be here to do my share"(379).

III *Information and Insight*

The Macmillan edition of *King Coal* includes a laudatory introduction by Georg Brandes, the influential Danish literary critic, who
cited three admirable aspects of the novel: its resemblance to Zola's
Germinal in power and concern, the strong protagonist with his
"great sympathy for the downtrodden," and Sinclair's "poetic
attitude" which is best shown in the "wonderful grace" he gives to
Mary Burke, who seems like "a Celtic Madonna . . . always ready to
fight for the worker's right"(xxi). Brandes's blurb may have won
readers for Sinclair in 1917, but it is not a penetrating analysis of the
novel. Coexisting with obvious weaknesses, the real strengths of *King
Coal* lie in its dedication to factual information, its absence of
propaganda, its use of characters who have realistic inner conflicts in
addition to idealized qualities, and its thematic maturity.

Sinclair's primary intention in the novel was to present the facts of
life, work, and politics in coal-mining camps. The use of fiction,
which allowed him to concentrate in one setting events which had
actually occurred in different camps, is evidence of this intention.
The preeminent fact in *King Coal,* around which the rest of the
information clusters, is the complete and illegal control of workers by
the coal companies. The community at North Valley is a closed camp;
whatever contact the workers have with the outside world is furtive.
Union organizers are denied access to the miners, and since the
G.F.C. is a Republican company, Democratic politics have no place
in North Valley. The people there are not even free to purchase U. S.
postal money orders: they must buy company drafts. Perhaps the
most serious aspect of company control is the way officials either
prevent responsible and independent newspaper reporters from
entering the camp or make sure that these reporters see only what
the company wants them to see. These incriminating facts are more
than obvious in the story; to insure their acceptance as fact, Sinclair
quotes in a postscript a decision made by the Colorado Supreme
Court which substantiates most of his charges about the iron control
of coal companies.

If *King Coal* is strong in facts, it is refreshingly weak in propaganda.
There is Socialism in the story—several of the workers hope vaguely
for it—but it is not Hal Warner's creed. The hero may become a

Socialist in the future, but unlike Mary Abbott of the *Sylvia* novels or even Jurgis Rudkus of *The Jungle*, Hal does not argue for any particular doctrine besides social justice. He is, in fact, skeptical even of labor unions at the beginning of the story; and although he is converted to a belief in unions, his labor politics are evolutionary instead of revolutionary. The only explicit advertisement for Socialism in the novel occurs in the postscript, where it is unobtrusively presented as industrial democracy: "The citizens and workers of such industrial communities [the mining camps] . . . . will find that they have neither peace or freedom until they have abolished the system of production for profit, and established in the field of industry what they are supposed to have already in the field of politics—a government of the people, by the people, for the people"(395).

Despite the lack of blatant propaganda, the novel often suggests a fairly radical ideological bias. In some of Sinclair's earlier works—the last part of *The Jungle*, for instance—he affirms the ability of the upper class to lead the social revolution, mild or otherwise. But the relationship between Hal Warner and Mary Burke in *King Coal* casts doubt on the capacity of the elite to escape their class consciousness. In addition to this tinge of pessimism, which implies that the working class must make its own revolution, Sinclair allows one of the miners to voice an even more pessimistic opinion when he draws an analogy between the workers' struggle and ants who cross a chasm by filling it up with their own bodies until a bridge is formed (108). Such ideas, supported rather than denied by the plot of the novel, advance a case against Sinclair's own optimistic utopianism (as explained in *The Industrial Republic*) and against nonrevolutionary, paternalistic reform. Whether one can sense in the novel a subtle plea for a harder headed Marxism than Sinclair had ever before suggested is at least debatable.

Such considerations of the novel's political content indicates that its rhetoric is more respectable than many other Sinclair novels. It lacks the powerful, despairingly naturalistic tone of *The Jungle*; the plot seems extraordinarily coincidental when Hal's fiancée shows up in the coal region; and the young hero is abnormally mature in his interests and abilities. But in spite of these quite apparent flaws and one critic's stronger admiration for *Love's Pilgrimage*,[14] *King Coal* is the best work of fiction produced by Sinclair from 1907 to 1927.

Any criticism of *King Coal* should include Sinclair's failure to link up his two plots: the story of industrial conditions and an impromptu strike, and the story of Hal Warner's conflicting responses to two young women of different social classes. *King Coal* would be a better novel if Hal's political activities in North Valley had been more obviously motivated by—or at least related to—his feelings for Mary Burke. Instead, one gains the impression that Hal's political efforts would have been no different even if there had never been an attractive and outspoken proletarian girl at the camp. It is illuminating to note that in Zola's *Germinal* the strike leader's activities are closely tied up with his emotional response to the daughter of a French miner. Does this mean that Sinclair added the love plot merely to broaden the appeal of his novel?

A negative answer is implied by the lack of a sentimental resolution in Hal's love affairs. The parallel absence of a denouement in the labor plot is understandable: Sinclair treats facts, and the facts themselves were unresolved when he wrote the novel. But there is no comparable reason for the lack of clues to what will happen when Hal returns to upper-class life and to Jessie Arthur. When Jessie last appears in the story Hal knows that he still loves her. Yet he also recognizes grave differences between her and himself—differences which would certainly make it impossible for him to "fight for the working people" and be Jessie's husband at the same time. Hal might try to convert her to a real concern for workers, but Sinclair seems to deny such a possibility when he stresses Jessie's well hidden but firm prejudice against lower classes. A likely sequel to the adventures at North Valley would be a gradual weakening of Hal's convictions and sympathies after marrying Jessie. Such an ending is only a guess; Sinclair gives us no clues. On one hand Hal is determined at the end of the novel to "fight" for the workers; on the other he is almost hypocritically determined to return to Jessie rather than to act on his admitted strong feelings for Mary Burke. Sinclair, with the editorial assistance of his wife, opens up the heart of Hal Warner and reveals a serious and significant conflict. But he refuses to sew his hero up and let the reader see the results of the conflict in Hal's life.

What this ambivalence indicates, besides a lack of [aesthetic] control, is that by 1917 Sinclair's ideas concerning the social responsibility of individuals had grown less simplistic. Throughout the story, not only in the feelings of Hal Warner, the author acknowledges a conflict between the claims of social responsibility and the satisfactions, however meager, of the status quo. The conflict occurs, for instance, in the home of Jerry Minetti, where Hal rooms. Minetti is a Socialist, but his Socialist goals are always compromised by the small affluence that his job provides in spite of hardships. Mary Burke, too, feels a conflict. On one hand the bitterness which she feels towards life in the mining camps is a source of near revolutionary solidarity, especially when she leads the miners in the strike; on the other hand, she begs Hal to take her, alone, away from North Valley. Others in the story have similar feelings. When Hal must organize a "conspiracy" to support him for check-weighman, he is forced to draw upon those workers who do not have family responsibilities. In these manifestations of Sinclair's theme of individual social responsibility, the author's developing sense of complexity is evident, for nowhere does he explicitly condemn those individuals who do not choose social responsibility over individual economic or emotional needs. He clearly admires those who can make the choice at times—like Hal Warner—but he also suggests that the same person may not always be able to stay on the narrow path of idealism when emotional needs or class prejudices interfere with his forward movement.

CHAPTER 6

War and Its Aftermath

IF Sinclair had been as much a part of the American literary
avant-garde in the twenties as he had been in 1906, he would have
shipped out for Europe or started writing of modern life as a
wasteland. He did neither. Although it was often dented, his idealism
served him well as a shield against disillusionment in the post-war
decade. He did not participate in what historians have identified as a
pervasive shift from pre-1914 "innocence" to a deepening sense of
complexity in the twenties, to an awareness that the "central
meaning" of the world "was neither clean nor cheerful."[1] Instead,
Sinclair was generally successful in retaining his older, progressive,
and politically radical attitudes. As Walter Rideout says in his book on
American radical novels, in "the lonely twenties" Sinclair "almost
was radical American literature."[2]

Yet Rideout's statement should not be read to mean that Sinclair
was completely unchanged by what he saw happening between 1914
and 1930. In fact, the title of one of his later Lanny Budd novels
identifies the twenties as an epoch "Between Two Worlds," an era
lacking the stability and certainty of earlier times. Sinclair himself
was considerably affected by the war and its political repercussions.
The great conflict showed him that even the Socialist Party was
fallible, and the fading away of radical political interest afterwards in
America forced him to rely increasingly on his own perceptions and
experiences.

Between *King Coal* in 1917 and the publication of *Oil!* in 1927,
with the Socialist movement in retreat, the nature of Sinclair's efforts
as a writer changed in two ways. The most obvious shift was in the
direction of more nonradical writing, a change indirectly related to
World War I. Because Sinclair no longer had his pre-war sense of
participation in a major collective movement, he was free to devote
much of his energy to such non-radical causes as prohibition and

92

psychic phenomena. These and other interests, treated at length in a didactic prescriptive work called the *Book of Life* (1922), were also a result of two other factors: his separation from the locus of American intellectual life in New York City after 1914 and, beginning in 1918, his decision to publish his own books in Pasadena.[3]

The other shift in Sinclair's writing from 1917 to 1927 is apparent in his almost experimental approaches to serious social criticism. In fiction Sinclair tended to turn away from propaganda directed at specific political needs and towards more general indictments of American capitalism, often relying on fantasy as a rhetorical vehicle and avoiding the direct depiction of social reality that he had used in *The Jungle* and *King Coal*. In nonfiction he began explaining the role of capitalism in religion, journalism, education, and art by relying extensively on his own personal experience in each area. Both Sinclair's fiction and his nonfiction during this period are weaker in quality than in quantity, giving the impression not only of experiment, but also of groping, of trying to find both his voice and an audience in post-war America. In general, his career from 1917 to 1927 was a period of transition between his earlier role as spokesman for the American Socialist movement and his later role as an independent anti-capitalist critic.

I Jimmie Higgins

Sinclair's reactions to World War I were determined more by pragmatic assessments of events than by ideology. As the conflict developed from 1914 to 1917 he was divided between the Socialist injunction to refuse cooperation with any capitalist government involved in war, and his fear of German militarism. His first published statement on the subject of international war had been in 1909 when he published "War: A Manifesto against It" in *Wilshire's Magazine* and contended that "war between civilized nations was the crime of crimes." Sinclair was not advocating pacifism, however, and he took pains to explain that he would never be able to "denounce all wars." Yet the brunt of his manifesto was that any war would make a large scale social revolution (by nonviolent means) more difficult to manage.[4] This message had to be modified after 1914 when Sinclair decided that the German military machine had to be crushed before the international Socialist movement could continue. He was particulary persuaded in this matter by his friend Frederick Van Eeden, a Dutch poet who supplied him with vivid details of events in Europe; by George D. Herron, who was in Italy; and by the exiled

Russian prince, Peter Kropotkin.[5] Consequently, he refused to join the anti-war movement that was building among radicals in the United States.

When the United States entered the war in 1917, Sinclair broke with the Socialist Party and supported Woodrow Wilson's war policy. After the Armistice, when he learned that American troops were being used to put down the Bolshevik Revolution, he switched from his short-lived nationalism back to his anti-capitalist stance. All of these shifts are reflected in *Jimmie Higgins*, his 1919 novel of the war.

In July 1917 Sinclair decided to resign from the Socialist Party because it opposed America's entrance into the war. In his public letter of resignation he stated his belief that the autocracy of Germany could be defeated by force, that force is often as necessary as it was in the American Civil War, and that radicals should work for a successful settlement of the war rather than indiscriminately oppose all governments. "I intend to go on working for Socialism as hard as I can," he wrote, "and when this crisis is past, when the breakdown of the Prussian caste system seems to me to have progressed far enough, I may come back and ask you to take me in again."[6]

The chief way in which Sinclair continued to work for Socialism was by starting his own radical journal in 1918. The title of his publication was *Upon Sinclair's*; it was subtitled, at first, *A Monthly Magazine: For a Clean Peace and the Internation.* By "Internation" Sinclair meant a Wilsonian international body which could guarantee self-government to the people of every country. *Upton Sinclair's*, written almost entirely by its namesake except for correspondence and reports from others, was published throughout 1918 and into 1919 until Sinclair found the journal financially impossible and settled instead for a weekly page in the *Appeal to Reason* for the next several years. While it lasted, the monthly publication was a significant (there were ten thousand subscribers at one point) adventure in personal journalism that tried to walk a precarious fence between support of the President's war policy and support for fellow radicals who were agitating for free speech and against militarism.[7]

Beginning late in the summer of 1918, Sinclair grew increasingly disturbed over reports of American troops sent to Archangel to help suppress the Bolshevik Revolution. In August he sent Wilson a telegraph pleading for noninterference.[8] In the winter, after he began to get detailed reports on Russia from Albert Rhys William and John Reed,[9] who had observed the Bolshevik takeover, his published outcries took a harder line. Finally, in January 1919 in the pages of his journal he warned that a violent revolution might even seem justified in America if the government did not tend to its own affairs and leave the Bolsheviks alone. Only "a speedy and ungrudging concession of the workers' demands for the full product of their labor and the full control of the conditions of their labor" could then prevent a takeover of Wall Street and Fifth Avenue by "the half million Jews emerging from the East Side" and a takeover of American industry by its workers.[10]

While Sinclair was trying to understand the war and American military policy in Russia during 1918, he was also writing a novel about the same material. *Jimmie Higgins,* written and serially published (in *Upton Sinclair's* and elsewhere) throughout 1918 and then issued as a book without revisions, documents the ambivalent attitudes that many American radicals felt towards World War I. Sinclair attempts to credit the United States for its opposition to militarism in most of his narrative, but, in the end, he suggests that American policy primarily and wrongly supports capitalism.

The novel concerns an ordinary rank and file member of the Socialist Party named Jimmie Higgins who, like Sinclair, eventually decides that he must fight against the German menace. At first Jimmie accepts the Socialist line of nonparticipation in the military efforts of a capitalist nation. But when he learns that German militarism is a threat to international Socialism and that German agents are even at work in the United States, he begins to agree with a Romanian Jewish friend who tells him that the Socialist revolution can wait a year or two while German militarism is being defeated. Furthermore, he learns from an old farmer that America has a strong radical tradition (expressed both in the Revolution and in the anti-slavery movement). As a result he "takes the plunge" and joins the army, distinguishing himself in battle until he discovers that he is part of an American expedition to Archangel in Russia. Not understanding why it is necessary for America to put down the Russian Revolution after the defeat of Germany, Jimmie dissents—and is tortured into insanity for doing so. In the closing chapters of the novel, after portraying the American military sympathetically in France, Sinclair asserts that military leaders have wrongly convinced Woodrow Wilson that involvement in Russia is necessary to save the world from violent revolution.

In addition to being an important document (of American radicalism as well as of Sinclair's political attitudes), *Jimmie Higgins* was also important in Sinclair's literary development. In particular,

since he took an ordinary worker as his protagonist (the name Jimmie
Higgins was often used generically to refer to rank and file Socialists),
his war novel meant a temporary return to the basic technique of *The
Jungle*: documenting the oppressive conditions of capitalism in the
life of an industrial worker rather than leading an essentially genteel
character (Alan Montague in *The Metropolis*, Sylvia Castleman in the
Sylvia novels, Hal Warner in *King Coal*) into an awareness of
injustice. Although Jimmie Higgins is already a Socialist when the
story begins, he resembles Jurgis Rudkus more than any other
Sinclair protagonist.

As in *The Jungle*, Sinclair strives with considerable but artless
effort in *Jimmie Higgins* to create shock and horror. Industrial
violence, murder, castration, agonizing death in battle, torture, and
brainwashing all have their place in the narrative. The following
description of a battle wound is typical of Sinclair's often gruesome
focusing: "The leader continued exhorting them; until suddenly an
annoying thing happened—right in the midst of his shouting, the
whole of his mouth and jaw disappeared. You did not see what
became of it—it just vanished into nothingness, and there in the
place of it was a red cavern, running blood. The man stood with his
startled eyes shining white in his black and hairy face, and gurgling
noises coming out—as if he thought he was still shouting, or could if
he tried harder."[11] The effectiveness of this passage is actually
diminished by overemphasis and by the facetious irony of the word
annoying in the first sentence (which puts Sinclair's ironic and
rhetorical voice between the reader and the violent reality), but it
illustrates Sinclair's turn from the kind of well-wrought narrative he
attempted (under George Brett's advice) in *King Coal* to the
presentation of hard, brutal, and pointed facts in *Jimmie Higgins*.

Unfortunately, the story shifts too often with the shifting attitudes
of its author and too often suggests his intrusive presence between
reader and experience. It is not an especially readable novel today as
a result, and once Jimmie makes his decision to join the army, it does
not deal effectively with Sinclair's dominant theme of an individual's
relationship to his community. The kind of inner tension which
Sinclair suggests and the reader often feels in Jurgis Rudkus and Hal
Warner is largely missing from Jimmie Higgins, who in more than
one sense is sacrificed to the excitement of war.

II *Into the Twenties*

Jimmie Higgins suggests that by 1919 many of Sinclair's basic
radical instincts had survived the war. He had briefly flirted with

nationalism and at times had expressed a belief that American policy would support democratic processes at home and abroad. After America's intervention in Russia, he began again to doubt the inevitability of democracy and social justice in American politics, and he regained his faith in the Socialist movement. In spite of the protagonist's death, *Jimmie Higgins* closes on a note of radical certainty: "In the industrial troubles which are threatening the great democracy of the West, there will appear men and women animated by a fierce and blazing bitterness; and the great democracy of the West will marvel at their state of mind, unable to conceive what can have caused it" (282).

The problem with this kind of assertion was that the opposite seemed to be happening. American radicalism tended to fade out after the war. Warren Harding's stated desire for "normalcy" fell on many receptive ears, a great number of Americans grew increasingly opposed to anything which seemed even vaguely associated with the recent successful revolution in Russia, and the pre-war force of progressive politics quickly dwindled into support for prohibition. Many left-leaning intellectuals and writers tended to straighten up after the war, largely because the Bolsheviks demonstrated that utopia would be achieved through violence rather than by an ascension of individual freedom or by the influence of rhetoric on the masses. (This statement should not imply that Sinclair believed that the Bolshevik way was the only way to achieve social revolution. Although the Bolsheviks were the only revolutionaries who had successfully created a Socialist state, he argued that nonviolent methods would work in America.) Finally, late in 1919 the antithesis of Sinclair's revolutionary dreams occurred when Attorney General A. Mitchell Palmer began his "red raids" against suspected alien subversives, trampling on civil rights in the process and arresting ten thousand persons, many of whom were not even members of radical organizations.

For Sinclair the temper of American life in the early twenties was both a purgative and a corrosive influence on his serious writing. His fiction and his nonfiction during these years reveal a weakening of certainty and, consequently, a heightened awareness of injustice and irrationality in American life. But his works also reveal a subtle yet disturbing flight from reality evident in a number of rhetorical manifestations: facetiousness, fantasy, and (especially in nonfiction) an excessive dependence on personal rather than objective information. This tension between realistic content and rhetorical evasion is especially apparent in *100%* (1920) and *They Call Me Carpenter*

(1922), Sinclair's major ventures in fiction between *Jimmie Higgins* and the highly successful achievement of *Oil!* in 1927.

Subtitled "The Story of a Patriot," *100%* deals with false patriotism and anti-radical hysteria. Obviously written in response to the Palmer raids, the novel expresses Sinclair's fear that such anti-radical and anti-immigrant feeling was becoming a permanent part of American life. His approach to this problem was through artless but hardboiled satire. The facetious blurb which he wrote for the dust jacket of his novel (which he published himself) can stand as a synopsis:

> Would you like to go behind the scenes and watch the leaders of your country saving you from the Reds?
>
> The author of "The Jungle" and "The Brass Check," chastened by the war, has hung up his "muck rake" for the time, and presents a study of loyalty and vital service.
>
> The hero of this book is a 100% American; a red-blooded patriot, a "he-man" and no mollycoddle. He becomes a secret agent, an "undercover operative," and we are shown from the inside the methods whereby the Bolshevik has been fought down and the country delivered from the Red Terror. [12]

100% is thus a story about a man who deserves no sympathy from a liberal or radical audience and who therefore shows little sign of inner conflicts.

The novel is unique in its exploration of the power of nonrational enthusiasm (patriotism) to corrupt rationality. The red-blooded hero is Peter Gudge, who for the sake of money—and out of background of wandering criminality and viciousness—engages in violence against radicals and thereby becomes a respected citizen. The money paid to Gudge is, of course, supplied by Big Business, and the radicals who appear in the story tend to be paradigms of benevolence. The attack in *100%* is not totally political, however. Such aspects of American life as jazz and alcohol are heavily condemned: dancing to jazz music, for instance, is portrayed as a fantastic and animalistic ritual involving "half-naked goddesses" and "black-coated gods" (130). Sinclair's main target is the combination of patriotism and capitalism which finally becomes a "religion" to Gudge and allows him to continue his anti-radical binge "in the sacred name of patriotism and the still more sacred name of democracy" (118).

This kind of social criticism, implying that democracy and patriotism in America are mere facades behind which hide exploitation and violence, is unusually strong even for Sinclair. The fact that *100%* contains no explicit plea for political action and fails to imply an impending turn towards Socialism, the "golden dawn of the new day" which Walter Rideout has identified as a dominant motif in pre-World War I radical novels in America,[13] adds more than a note of bitterness to the tone of the novel. Yet the story of Peter Gudge, even with Sinclair's substitution of violent reactionary behavior for imminent revolution, is not deeply pessimistic. Rather, it is an exercise in Socialistic fantacizing about weak-minded conservativism rather than a credible depiction of social ills. The commitment to real facts, to experience as it is, the quality that made *The Jungle* a best seller in 1906, is missing from *100%*.

They Call Me Carpenter (1922) is also a seriously flawed story, but for somewhat different reasons. The problem this time involves an odd contradiction, in the tone of the novel, between levity and seriousness. The consistent seriousness of *The Jungle* or *Jimmie Higgins* is gone. Instead, in *They Call Me Carpenter* Sinclair oscillates between fantasy and facetiousness on one hand, and tragic political implications on the other. *They Call Me Carpenter* conveys the impression that its author was on the verge of a loss of political faith in America and therefore retreated into sometimes facetious satire as a temporary stay against confusion.

The story is cleverly imaginative. It begins when the narrator, named Billy, is attacked and beaten by a group of veterans who see him coming out of a theater where a futuristic German film is showing. Billy loses consciousness before the stained glass window of a church, and when he awakens he finds that the figure represented in the window is now standing beside him. Obviously Jesus, Billy's new friend, calls himself Carpenter. What is really important about Carpenter is his politics: he is an individualist, an anarchist who does not believe in government, and a firm believer in non-institutionalized brotherhood. That Carpenter's politics will not work in modern America becomes apparent when Billy introduces him to the labor problems of Western City, a fictional name for Los Angeles. At the end of the story, Carpenter decides that only by becoming a martyr can he personally help solve the political problems of Western City. But when he offers himself as martyr he is ridiculed, shamed, and brutalized by the populace to such an extent that he gives up the attempt and runs back to his safe but ineffective role in the stained glass window. At this point Billy realizes that the whole story has been a dream.[14]

There are two major rhetorical goals in *They Call Me Carpenter*.

The first is to show that America or "Mobland" as it is called in the
novel is controlled by violent groups of superpatriots like the
American Legion and the Ku Klux Klan. Sinclair's rhetoric is not
persuasive in conveying the malignity of such behavior because all of
the mobs in the story seem only to be part of a not very serious
fantasy. The second point of the book is to indicate that the ideals of
Jesus, which should have social implications, are now useless because
they have been appropriated by the conservative institution of the
church. Rather than a living creed, Christianity is merely something
to admire, a stained glass window which colors and blurs one's
perception of social reality. This understanding of Christianity, which
Sinclair had been shaping in his mind ever since adolescence, and
which he had articulated a few years previously in *The Profits of
Religion* (1918), counteracts the mediocrity of the novel's attempt to
depict social reality. The result is not good fiction, but the ideas in the
novel are perceptive, especially in view of the rise of fundamentalistic and nonpolitical Christianity throughout the 1920's.

III *Slapping the Dead Hand*

In emphasizing Sinclair's role as a novelist it is easy to slight his
other works. In his career during the early and middle twenties this
danger is especially likely. Although Sinclair produced several novels
during this period, the majority of his publications were nonfiction. A
list of all the books he published between 1918 and 1927 can illustrate
his prolific ventures in rhetoric:

Date of Publication	*Book*
October 1918	*The Profits of Religion* (nonfiction)
May 1919	*Jimmie Higgins* (novel)
January 1920	*The Brass Check* (nonfiction)
October 1920	*100%* (novel)
September 1921	*The Book of Life,* vol. I (nonfiction)
May 1922	*The Book of Life,* vol. II (nonfiction)
September 1922	*They Call Me Carpenter* (novel)
March 1923	*The Goose-Step* (nonfiction)
February 1924	*The Goslings* (nonfiction)
1924, month uncertain	*Singing Jailbirds* (play)
February 1925	*Mammonart* (nonfiction)
September 1925	*Bill Porter* (play)
April 1926	*Letters to Judd* (nonfiction)
August 1926	*The Spokesman's Secretary* (satire)
March 1927	*Oil!* (novel)
November 1927	*Money Writes!* (nonfiction)

All of these books were published by Sinclair himself, although some were issued simultaneously by commercial firms.

The non-novels on the list are of varying significance. *The Book of Life*—which includes four subordinate "books" dealing respectively with the mind, the body, love, and society—was Sinclair's attempt to tell his readers what he felt he knew and they needed to know in order to survive in modern society. Unfortunately, the high levels of didacticism and prescription (rather than observation and recording) as well as some rather strange advice render the book generally obsolete and occasionally ludicrous. (One of the more disturbing bits of advice in the book is Sinclair's suggestion that racial problems in America might be solved by dividing the nation into three racially defined areas: one for whites who want to preserve their "integrity of blood," one for blacks, and one for those who would like to try integration. Whites would get the industrial heartland of the nation, while blacks would get the agricultural Southeast.[15]) One of Sinclair's plays in the twenties, *Singing Jailbirds*, an expressionistic piece based on the author's own short incarceration for asserting his rights of free speech, was an effective dramatization of political oppression practiced against the American proletariat. The other play, *Bill Porter*, was an ineffective attempt to make an oppressed proletarian out of O. Henry. *Letters to Judd*, explanatory epistles on capitalism and Socialism written hypothetically to an old carpenter Sinclair knew in Pasadena, was a surprisingly popular book among lower- and lower-middle-class readers (it was circulated with the assistance of Ernest Haldeman-Julius in Girard, Kansas). *The Spokesman's Secretary*, also epistolary, was a feeble attempt to satirize Calvin Coolidge through letters written by a hypothetical semi-literate girlfriend of the President's secretary. The most important Sinclair books in the early and middle twenties were six analyses of capitalist institutions which he called his "Dead Hand" series.

By 1920 Upton Sinclair was not a popular author outside Socialist circles, and his manner of issuing his own books under his own imprint tended to restrict their propagation to the faithful. However, the "Dead Hand" books made him once again an important figure in American letters by presenting readable and iconoclastic attacks on capitalist institutions.[16] What Sinclair tried to show was the difference between the reality of a "Dead Hand" of greed in human life and the ideal of Adam Smith's laissez-faire concept of an "Invisible Hand" guiding economics. In *The Profits of Religion* he dealt with the abuse of institutionalized religion to support particular monarchs and economic classes throughout Western history. In *The Brass Check*, the most popular volume in the series and a book read admiringly even by Scott Fitzgerald, [17] Sinclair analyzed class bias in American journalism. In *The Goose-Step* he tried to show the obsequious relationship between higher education and capitalism (particularly in the form of specific industrialists or wealthy families). In *The Goslings* he tried to show that the same kind of relationship existed in American elementary and secondary education, especially in Roman Catholic schools. In *Mammonart* he explored class bias in literature and art, pointing out that only a handful of artists since Homer have failed to serve the prevailing and oppressive economic establishment (artists whom Sinclair finds reason to admire on his ideological grounds include Euripides, Dante, Michelangelo, Cervantes, Milton, Bunyan, Molière, Swift, Whitman, Nietzsche, and Tolstoy; those whom Sinclair criticizes for their support of oppressive regimes include, surprisingly, Shakespeare, Dostoevski, Conrad, and many others who have also been universally admired.) Finally, in *Money Writes!* Sinclair applied his analysis to recent writing and found most of his contemporaries lacking in the proper radical perspectives.

Something on the order of *The Brass Check* was needed in 1920 to argue that the Associated Press tended to obtain its information on subjects such as labor violence primarily from the spokesmen of capital; and *Mammonart* is still an interesting book of opinions, some quite witty, which also defines Sinclair's idea of the role of an artist (his work, he says, is largely in the spirit of Whitman's *Democratic Vistas* [18]). But flaws in the "Dead Hand" series are numerous and widespread. In the first place the books are unwilling to admit that any forces beyond economics are at work in civilization. Also, all of them (but the works on education in particular) rely on a conspiratorial theory of history in which monarchs or plutocrats are always conscious agents of corruption or oppression. Finally, in general they lack specific and concrete evidence for many charges; Sinclair bases most of his conclusions on personal experience, relating in especial detail his unfortunate adventures in religion, journalism, and education. As one scholar says, "in none of these six books did Sinclair document the countless indictments of capitalist culture. The reader simply has to accept Sinclair's word that he had never knowingly published a falsehood."[19]

In spite of their weaknesses the "Dead Hand" books, which required prodigious research and correspondence (Sinclair recorded sixty thousand words of interview notes while researching higher education), meant more to Sinclair and his career than publicity and a wider readership. They meant extensive contact with American life and serious consideration of political and economic ideas. Most of all they meant purging himself of a long germinating desire to analyze—within his conspiratorial and neo-Marxian framework—institutions which he felt allowed some men to overpower other men, a desire indicated as early as 1911 in the pages of *Love's Pilgrimage*. Once he had satisfied this desire, he could move on to two complex and important novels, *Oil!* and *Boston,* in 1927 and 1928 respectively.

CHAPTER 7

Literary Renascence: Oil!

"I TS curiosity and ease and power are Tolstoyan." This evaluation was offered of *Oil!* by Floyd Dell, both a friend and a critic of Sinclair's, at the time the novel was published in 1927.[1] Dell was not alone in his opinion, for reviewers in general realized that Sinclair's new story of Southern California, petroleum entrepreneurship, and American culture was a work to be taken seriously and was a refreshing departure from the kind of writing Sinclair had been doing since the end of World War I. Echoing Dell, the reviewer in the *Independent* wrote that although Sinclair was still a propagandist at times in his novel, "the significant thing about the book is the degree to which a sheer knowledge of certain strands of American life and a certain gusto in telling about them swamp the special pleader."[2] In the *New Republic* William McFee recognized that *Oil!* revealed Sinclair's natural métier: "Those of us who lose patience with Mr. Sinclair as a propagandist, who have read his fanatical nonsense in 'The Brass Check,' in 'The Goose Step' and, above all, in 'Mammonart,' will rejoice to discover that a man can be a fine novelist and a crazy fanatic at the same time. This does not mean that his skill as a novelist derives from his craziness as a fanatic. Upton Sinclair is a novelist because he cannot help himself."[3] These statements indicate that in 1927 Sinclair suddenly gave signs of behaving like the writer that intelligent readers had long expected him to be; he had written a serious novel that captured identifiable and empathetic experience on a remarkably broad canvas.

I *American Panorama*

Oil! was loosely based on the oil scandals of the Harding administration. Beginning in early 1924 Sinclair started thinking about building a novel around the Teapot Dome events. He may have first considered another muckraking novel on the order of *The Jungle* or *King Coal* which would deal with specific and recognizable figures and present a plot only slightly changed from front-page reality. Fortunately, between 1924 and 1927 he developed another novelistic approach combining the best features of *The Jungle* or *King Coal* with a few narrative innovations. The result was a story which took as its ostensible main character an upper-class youth much like Hal Warren of his coal story, contrasted this elite protagonist with the parallel development of a working-class and eventually radical youth only vaguely like Jurgis Rudkus or Jimmie Higgins, and spread the narrative over at least as many years as he had used in *The Jungle.* To this basic pattern he added personal conflicts, especially involving the elite protagonist's feelings for his father, and devised his plot to include excursions into such aspects of American life as Hollywood lifestyles, internal problems created by World War I, political corruption, strikes, industrial accidents, revivals, seances, Bolsheviki, football games, and flappers. That Sinclair only required six hundred pages for his story may be an achievement in itself.

Consequently, an attempt to summarize the novel does it an injustice. The basic plot concerns Bunny Ross and his oilman father, J. Arnold Ross, generally referred to as "Dad." J. Arnold Ross is a semi-literate but quickly rising figure in the Southern California oil game, and his son (a teenager when the story begins) admires both him and his practicality until he accidentally meets Paul Watkins, the son of a poverty stricken rancher. Paul is intelligent, is becoming educated, and is developing radical sympathies. He galvanizes Bunny's idealism and helps create Bunny's continual problem of deciding whether he should be in favor of liberal action which he knows to be just, or in favor of conventional action which he knows his father will approve.

As the story progresses Paul becomes increasingly radical, especially after serving in World War I and being forced to fight against Bolsheviks in Russia, and Bunny mingles with wealthy young women, including a movie star, while struggling with his social conscience. The elder Ross, generous at heart and willing to understand as much as he can about his son's and even Paul's ideas but forced by a federation of oilmen and his own pride to resist labor unions and eventually support political corruption, grows richer, older, and less happy. Much of the action in *Oil!* occurs in the oilfields on what was once merely the Watkins ranch, where Paul becomes a leader of the workers and Bunny becomes a liberal sympathizer and financially supports a Socialist journal. Paul has a sister, Ruth, who admires and follows him; and a brother, Eli, who becomes a famous and quite rich revivalist.

Unlike *The Jungle, Oil!* does not arrive at a tidy but artificial ending. J. Arnold Ross dies of a heart attack and Bunny begins increasingly to weigh his social idealism against the possible recourse of violence which Paul, finally a Communist, has accepted as necessary to insure social justice. Bunny is opposed both to capitalism and to the Third International; vaguely, he hopes that Socialism can offer a nonviolent way out. But he uncovers no facts to justify his hope. Instead, he sees Paul Watkins murdered by a right wing mob and after his death learns of the suicide of Paul's sister. In the last paragraph of the novel Sinclair attempts ideologically to pin the tragedies of the story solely on capitalist greed:

You can see those graves, with a picket fence about them, and no derrick for a hundred feet or more. Some day all those unlovely derricks will be gone, and so will the picket fence and the graves. There will be other girls with bare brown legs running over those hills, and they may grow up to be happier women, if men can find some way to chain the black and cruel demon which killed Ruth Watkins and her brother—yes, and Dad also: an evil Power which roams the earth, crippling the bodies of men and women, and luring the nations to destruction by visions of unearned wealth, and the opportunity to enslave and exploit labor.[4]

By this point, however, a reader is primarily aware only of the death, whatever its ultimate cause, of three convincingly developed characters.

There are weaknesses and false steps in *Oil!* but they are not as disturbing as in many of Sinclair's earlier works. The author often preaches to his readers, as he tries to do in the last paragraph, but he mostly narrates. Some characters—Eli Watkins in particular, but also some of Bunny's girlfriends—are cardboard cutouts from the social history of the twenties, but the main figures are more than two-dimensional. Perhaps the most annoying aspect of the book is Sinclair's usual cliché-ridden style. Trying to describe Bunny's adolescent infatuation with an early high school girlfriend, Sinclair awkwardly writes, "It made Bunny walk on air, just to buy a new straw-hat, and meet his chosen one upon the street, and anticipate her comments!" (109).

Such failures of diction are offset by characterization. For the first time in his career as a novelist, in *Oil!* Sinclair was able to portray most of his characters—proletarian and plutocratic—with detachment. His usual dichotomy of good and evil, black and white, idealist and capitalist, is largely missing. As a reviewer in the *Nation* noticed, Sinclair had "at last realized the truth of Fielding's observation that 'we can censure the action without conceiving any absolute detestation of the person.' "[5] This kind of portrayal is particularly true in the cases of both Bunny Ross and his father. Bunny, although he is an obvious idealist and demonstrates many of his author's attitudes (albeit in a rather compromising situation), is not the youth of complete virtue that, say, Hal Warner is in *King Coal*. In fact, Bunny Ross is the first protagonist to engage in extramarital affairs that Sinclair portrays sympathetically—an aspect of characterization which encouraged the Boston chief of police to ban *Oil!* in that city.

Effective characterization is even more apparent in "Dad" Ross, the first hard-headed capitalist in a Sinclair novel to be depicted as a likeable and understandable person. J. Arnold Ross is appealing primarily because Bunny and Paul respond to both his generosity and power, and because Sinclair is careful to show that he is not free of inner conflicts. His drive for wealth and his use of power are clearly understood as the result of a broken heart incurred when his first wife divorced him on the grounds of insufficient affluence. As Michael Millgate points out in *American Social Fiction*, Ross is a believable and intriguing businessman:

Surprisingly enough it is Upton Sinclair, in his portrait of J. Arnold Ross in *Oil!* (1927), who comes as near as anyone to embodying Van Wyck Brooks's conception of the businessman [as interesting and deserving of literary treatment]. In Sinclair's early novels businessmen appear either as shadowy abstractions, as in *The Jungle* (1906), or as monster-like caricatures, as in *The Metropolis* (1908). In *Oil!*, no less than in these early books, Sinclair remains uncompromisingly committed against all that Ross, the oil-man, represents; nevertheless he deliberately presents Ross as possessing qualities of personal attractiveness which emerge the more strongly from this context of economic hostility. Even the communists, we learn, respect businessmen of Ross's kind: they have power and do not hesitate to use it; they play the game for all they are worth. Paul Watkins, fighting to take away the power of the oil-men, does not in the least blame them for fighting to hold on to it.[6]

That Ross's character becomes more attractive in a "context of economic hostility" is a clue to the historical uniqueness of *Oil!* As he had frequently done before, Sinclair failed to follow prevailing literary trends in *Oil!* Whereas many of the best novelists in the twenties—Hemingway, Fitzgerald, Lewis—were revolting from the

village and attacking middle-class American provinciality, Sinclair
chose to ignore the middle class, reveal the nature of the economic
plutocracy, and explore sources of admiration in the working class.
Since Sinclair focused on industrial workers to the exclusion of both a
much poorer rural population and American blacks, his workers are
actually the lower class on its way to attaining middle-class status. Yet
it is clear that the image of American life projected by Hemingway,
Lewis, *et al*,—of middle-class commercial workers and professionals,
properly genteel and living in small towns or possessing small town
mentalities—had little appeal for Sinclair in the 1920's. He was still a
true believer in the Socialist dichotomy of rich and poor, and would
remain so for a while longer.

In another departure from advanced literary trends in the
twenties, Sinclair chose to write fiction about America itself.
Expatriates in Europe were far from his consciousness. Instead, he
wrote from a set of native assumptions about the nature of America
and the necessity to make it conform with dreams and expectations.
Social tensions, economic forces, and political ideals are the stuff of
Oil! Sinclair's novel is closer to the concerns of American fiction in the
thirties than it is to that of the twenties. In writing the book Sinclair
was particularly aware of the agony of class differences and of the
serious difficulties of resolving them.

Consequently, violence is a major aspect of the novel. *Oil!* does not
necessarily contain more violent scenes than other Sinclair novels
(*Jimmie Higgins* has a much greater quantity of violence within its
pages), but its violence is less mitigated by ideological optimism,
often understated, and more impressive. In one early scene in J.
Arnold Ross's oilfield a roughneck named Joe Gundha, never before
mentioned in the story, falls into a well and drowns in the mud.
Sinclair resists the temptation to describe the procedure of bringing
the body up with a grappling hook, but gives this single death a sense
of importance by having it remain in the minds and consciousness of
other characters. Bunny, for example, ponders the significance of
Gundha's death in the following manner: "Yes, life was strange—and
cruel. You lived in the little narrow circle of your own consciousness,
and, as people said, what you didn't know didn't hurt you. Your
Thanksgiving dinner was spoiled, because one poor laborer had slid
down into a well which you happened to own; but dozens and perhaps
hundreds of men had been hurt in other wells all over the country,
and that didn't trouble you a bit" (151). Ruth Watkins is also
tormented by this death. At the end of the novel, after her brother

has been killed by the mob, it is Joe Gundha whom she remembers as she throws herself into the same hole that took his life.

More blatant kinds of violence in *Oil!* include oilfield fires, labor warfare, and the mobbing of a radical meeting where Paul Watkins is murdered. These individual episodes are subordinate to the sense of intrinsic violence which is unrelieved by any attempts at political hopefulness in the novel.

II *Individuals and Society*

More than any previous Sinclair novel, including both *The Jungle* and *King Coal, Oil!* presses Sinclair's major theme of the radical sensibility in conflict with community needs and with the expectations of responsibility. It does this by exploring the difficulty, in the lives of more than one character, of remaining a social idealist. The difficulty is present to some extent in J. Arnold Ross himself, but more obviously in Bunny and in Paul Watkins.

Bunny's problem is a combination of idealism and love of his father. His idealism begins with his acquaintance with Paul Watkins, who is at first no more than a poor youth who holds a special attraction for the wealthy and pampered Bunny by making him aware of poverty. Paul actually embodies overtones of Christian symbolism and later affects Bunny in a more than rational manner, although he never converts him to Communism. Near the end of the story Bunny "knew there was something unusual about his own devotion to Paul, the subjection of his mind to everything that Paul thought, the exactness of his memory of everything that Paul had said" (512). Paul is Bunny's personal messiah who "had given him an ideal" (513) and made him unsatisfied with money and pleasure.

Unfortunately, Bunny is not able to consistently or continually act on idealistic grounds. For years he suffers from moral lapses, particularly when women of his own class are involved, until he finally marries an intellectual daughter of the working class, Rachel Menzies. But he suffers more from his unwillingness to hurt his father. Not until four hundred pages into the story is he able to say to J. Arnold Ross, "I just can't let my love for any one person in the world take the place of my sense of justice" (414). Often Bunny's divided allegiances expand to include a tension between radical political perceptions and established "patriotic" stances. During World War I when he hears that the American expedition against Bolsheviks in Archangel has been checked, he is "torn between two sets of emotions," national loyalty and an urge "to cheer when the flag had to retreat" (255). Bunny Ross eventually becomes a complete convert to idealism and social justice, but the process of conversion requires the entire story; and even at the end he finds it disturbingly difficult to maintain his nonviolent Socialist posture in the face of a violent political scene. Much of this narrative echoes Sinclair's own difficulties when his commitment to both idealism and writing interfered painfully with his responsibilities as husband and provider in his first marriage, and when he tried to maintain his moderate, nonviolent radicalism in a political environment where the appeal of hard-boiled Communism was close and frequent. After 1929 Sinclair gave the dogmatic impression that he could easily maintain his essentially nineteenth century Socialism with its hopes for nonviolent revolution as evolution (often comparing his idea of social revolution to the hatching of an egg—a gradual evolutionary process up to a certain point, and then a sudden but externally unforced culmination), but *Oil!* suggests that for a while at least his stance was precarious.

In *Oil!* the problems that Paul Watkins experiences are external rather than internal. Although his education, begun by working for a free-thinking lawyer, separates him from his evangelistic brother and his simpleminded father, his suffering is primarily on the level of political oppression. Paul is a "big, powerful figure, clad in a blue shirt and khaki trousers held up by suspenders" (122) who is drafted into the army after trying to organize oil workers into a union. In the army he is sent to Archangel, where he is converted into a Bolshevik. His politics thereafter are nongenteel, as he readily admits: "Democracy is the goal—it's the only thing worth working for. But it can't exist till we've broken the struggle-hold of big business. That's a fighting job, and it can't be done by democracy" (416). Surprisingly, Sinclair offers no condemnation of Paul's Communism other than the radical's death, which has the effect of suggesting martyrdom.
death, which has the effect of suggesting martyrdom.

The death of both Paul Watkins and J. Arnold Ross in the story may have been Sinclair's manner of implying that only Bunny's nonviolent politics deserves serious consideration. Sinclair may have also decided to kill Paul so that he would not have to develop and resolve the complex set of feelings that a serious revolutionary like Paul would have to confront—for example, whether to take human life or to give up his political goals. Only a Malraux or a Mailer could have effectively carried the story into this region, and Sinclair's choice of death for Paul may have been wise. The ending is convincing, even with its lack of political resolution.

Oil! is one of Sinclair's most effective works of fiction. From it he was able to move immediately into the writing of another serious and powerful novel, *Boston*, his story of the Sacco and Vanzetti case. But never again was he able to reproduce the unique achievement of *Oil!*, its compelling narrative unified with a broad sweep of American social life and history.

CHAPTER 8

The Novelist as Publicist: Boston

IN his analysis of American writing in the decade following the First World War, Frederick J. Hoffman says that, "Only one event of the 1920's succeeded in arousing intellectuals of every kind of political loyalty: the arrest, trial, and execution of two Italian anarchists, Nicola Sacco and Bartolomeo Vanzetti."[1] Such an event would hardly have failed to arouse Sinclair, whose creativity since 1905 had been fueled amost exclusively by the facts of political and social oppression in America. His response to the Sacco-Vanzetti case was almost predictable: *Boston*, a two volume novel of almost eight hundred pages which he published in 1928, a year after the executions. Sinclair's novel was the best out of several published after 1927 which attempted to focus on the case of the two anarchists. It has been judged as "an exceptional production" and a work "in the first rank of historical novels."[2]

In the Sinclair canon, *Boston* is a cognate of *Oil!*: a long novel intended to reveal and publicize economic, social, and political facts of American life in the 1920's. Whereas *Oil!* was loosely based on the scandals of the Harding administration and presents significant aspects of popular culture and social history of the twenties, *Boston* was more directly based on a scandal involving a working-class tragedy reflecting political tensions and prejudices of the time.

I *Sacco and Vanzetti*

The case of Nicola Sacco, an Italian shoeworker, and Bartolomeo Vanzetti, an Italian fish peddler with intellectual proclivities, began with a violent payroll robbery in South Braintree, Massachusetts, an industrial suburb of Boston.[3] On April 15, 1920, two bandits fatally shot a paymaster and guard of the Slater and Morrill shoe factories and escaped with the sixteen thousand dollar payroll in an accomplice's car. At the time police were searching for two men who had staged a similar but unsuccessful robbery the previous December in neighboring Bridgewater. Since eyewitnesses identified the criminals in each case as Italians, police looked for suspicious Italians with access to a car. On May 5, 1920, they arrested Sacco and Vanzetti, who had accompanied a friend to pick up his car at a garage. Both men were armed when arrested. A few months later they were indicted for the South Braintree crime; in addition, Vanzetti was charged with the earlier Bridgewater attempt.

Of overwhelming significance in the case was the fact that the two Italians were radicals, members of an anarchist study club and were active propagandists. They pleaded innocent to the criminal charges, eventually explaining that they carried guns because of their anxiety over the recent "red raids" by Attorney General A. Mitchell Palmer, during which thousands of suspected radicals had been arrested and hundreds of aliens deported because of their political activities. Sacco and Vanzetti's foreignness and radicalism became major issues at their trial. As Felix Frankfurter stated in his book on the case, "By systematic exploitation of the defendants' alien blood, their imperfect knowledge of English, their unpopular social views, and their opposition to the war, the District Attorney invoked against them a riot of political passion and patriotic sentiment; and the trial judge connived at—one had almost written, cooperated in—the process."[4]

On July 14, 1921, after Vanzetti had been convicted of the Bridgewater crime in a seemingly prejudicial separate trial, he and Sacco were found guilty of the murders in South Braintree. The prosecution had made an elaborate attempt to identify the men through eyewitnesses—which were countered by a larger number of eyewitnesses presented by the defense—and to establish that Sacco's pistol could have fired one of the fatal bullets. Despite these contrivances, the conviction was based largely on the defendant's "consciousness of guilt"—their anxious behavior and contradictory statements, which suggested criminality. At their trial and afterwards Sacco and Vanzetti claimed that such a "consciousness" was caused by their fears of being prosecuted as radicals and of implicating their anarchist comrades.

For the next six years the Sacco-Vanzetti Defense Committee, which began as a small collection of Italian friends and anarchist sympathizers but which grew to include many persons of varying political faiths, worked vigorously for a new trial. They sought out and presented new evidence and new witnesses; explained contradictions and obvious deceptions in the prosecution's case; claimed that the trial judge was obviously prejudiced; and even offered a written confession for the crime by Celestino F. Madeiros, a young Portuguese criminal. They also prepared an elaborate brief demonstrating that the payroll robbery was most likely committed by Madeiros and an Italian gang of professional criminals rather than by two regularly employed men without criminal records. All of these appeals, however, were denied by the trial judge, Webster Thayer. The Defense Committee then went to the Supreme Judicial Court of Massachusetts, only to find that the higher court was limited by statute to deciding only on "matters of law" and not "matters of fact" such as new evidence. When the Committee appealed to the federal courts it found that Supreme Court justices were unwilling to interfere in the legal process of Massachusetts. Sacco and Vanzetti's last hope was executive clemency, which Governor Alvin T. Fuller refused to grant after a personal investigation and a review of the case by a special commission composed of the presidents of Harvard and M.I.T. and a retired state judge. Therefore, shortly after midnight on August 23, 1927, the two defendants were electrocuted at Charlestown Prison. Members of their Defense Committee and liberal sympathizers were certain that they had not been tried fairly. Most were equally certain of their innocence. Sacco and Vanzetti themselves, up to the time of their execution, apparently believed that they were victims of class persecution by the wealthy people of the Boston area.

As Hoffman has expressed it, for seven years the Sacco-Vanzetti case "was a *cause célèbre*, followed by all men who were not simple reactionaries or merely indifferent to problems of justice and law."[5] At the conviction of the two Italians in 1921 there were anti-American bombings and demonstrations throughout the world. During the lengthy period of appeals, as the defendants, particularly Vanzetti, studied English, wrote eloquent letters, and spoke feelingly to authorities and reporters, they were the touchstone of leftist sympathies in America. Few persons of social conscience could remain detached when they read such words as the following, a statement given by Vanzetti to a reporter several weeks before his death:

If it has not been for these things, I might have live out my life, talking at street corners to scorning men. I might have die, unmarked, unknown, a failure. Now we are not a failure. This is our career and our triumph. Never in our full life can we hope to do such work for tolerance, for joostice, for man's understanding of man, as now we do by an accident. Our words—our lives—pains—nothing! The taking of our lives—lives of a good shoemaker and a poor fish peddler—all! That last moment belong to us—that agony is our triumph.[6]

If the execution of the two men did not make them martyrs in everyone's eyes, it did at the very least indict Americans of insensitivity and injustice.

In American letters the Sacco-Vanzetti case was a call to arms, the source of "a flood of protest literature,"[7] much of it melodramatic, all of it indignant. "March on, O dago Christs," wrote Malcolm Cowley, "while we march on to spread your name abroad/like ashes in the winds of God."[8] The case prompted at least nine works of fiction, the best of which were John Dos Passos's *U.S.A.* trilogy and Sinclair's *Boston.* In reference to the impact of Sacco and Vanzetti on Dos Passos, who among American writers was the most passionately involved in their defense, G. Louis Joughin in *The Legacy of Sacco and Vanzetti* has said that "at the age of thirty-one, the full growth of his creative literary power coincided with his serious interest in a major social catastrophe."[9] Something quite similar happened to Upton Sinclair.

II   *Involvement*

Although Sinclair did not join the Sacco-Vanzetti Defense Committee until the spring of 1927,[10] he had followed the case with interest for several years. Although his politics, which tended towards state Socialism, were quite different from the philosophical anarchism of the two Italians, he had published a sympathetic article on Vanzetti as early as 1922, and in 1923 he had written a favorable review of an autobiographical memoir that Vanzetti had written in the first years of his imprisonment.[11] But the idea of a novel based on the case did not begin to take shape in his mind until June 1927 when he travelled to Boston to publicize *Oil!*

Sinclair made his trip in response to the banning of his novel by the Boston chief of police, who identified certain passages, especially one mentioning birth control, as indecent. Always looking for ways to publicize his work, Sinclair designed new editions of *Oil!* with fig leaf imprinted blank pages in place of those which the chief of police had found objectionable. He then sold these fig leaf editions by parading on Boston sidewalks sandwiched between advertising boards in the design of fig leaves. While engaged in this bizarre stunt, he visited Vanzetti in jail, where he found his early impressions confirmed. Vanzetti, he later stated, "was one of the wisest and kindest persons I ever knew, and I thought him as incapable of murder as I was."[12]

In order to make arrangements for the publication of *Money Writes!*, the sequel to *Mammonart* which he had written immediately after finishing *Oil!*, Sinclair returned to California. But on the night of August 22, 1927, after learning of the execution in Boston, he felt "that the world would want to know the truth about this case," and therefore he decided to write a "contemporary historical novel" that would present the available facts.[13] His first step was to return to Boston and collect information about Sacco and Vanzetti, their trials, and their appeals. Almost unavoidably, he also raked around in the muck of Boston society, learning of family quarrels, immorality among the elite, and financial manipulations. His sources for this kind of information were proper Bostonians who had joined the Sacco-Vanzetti defense. It was Sinclair's opinion that Boston society—composed of the holders of wealth and respect, and the molders of opinion—was largely corrupt and socially irresponsible, often immoral, and possibly culpable for the tragedy of Sacco and Vanzetti.

The final result of Sinclair's investigations was *Boston*. While in the end it was not a great popular success—it sold only twenty-five thousand copies in 1928—it was one of Sinclair's best and most objective attempts at using fiction to convey specific information that he felt had not been adequately publicized. *Boston* was more than the result of the author's interest in a historical event of enormous social significance and surprising reverberation; in spite of several apparent and typical weaknesses it was also another sign—after *Oil!*—of a maturity in artistic conception that many of Sinclair's earlier novels fail to demonstrate.

Although the novel relies heavily on the reader's awareness of the Sacco and Vanzetti case, the strength of *Boston* as a literary achievement lies chiefly in its plot. Sinclair had a ready-made string of events for his basic narrative, but he did more than merely record a complex, suspenseful, and tragic story that American society had fortuitously created. Rather, the narrative gives ample evidence of Sinclair's imagination and his ability to imply connections between ostensibly disparate events. The title reveals Sinclair's intention: to go through and beyond the Sacco-Vanzetti story and to explore the nature of Boston itself in both its upper and lower ranges of social and economic life.

The central structural device in *Boston* is its main character, who is neither Sacco nor Vanzetti but an elderly Bostonian, Cornelia Thornwell, who becomes personally involved with the case. Although Cornelia shares characteristics with several women who gave their sympathy, time, and money to the Defense Committee,[14] she is largely a fictional character, as are many of the upper-class Bostonians in the novel. However, she moves among many characters who bear their real-life names—including the two defendants, many of their supporters, Judge Thayer, Governor Fuller, and President Lowell of Harvard. Cornelia functions in the novel not only as a sympathetic central consciousness evaluating the Sacco-Vanzetti case, but as a bridge between the working and wealthy classes. Cornelia satisfies these roles by being an ex-governor's wife who, upon the death of her not quite beloved husband, rebels against wealth and propriety, becomes a "runaway grandmother," and seeks experience as a member of the working class. When she boards with an Italian family—after finding employment in a cordage factory once owned by her husband—she meets Bartolomeo Vanzetti. This meeting occurs several years before his arrest. Although she cannot agree completely with his anarchism, she is drawn to his compassionate nature and to his intellect. When he is arrested, Cornelia becomes his strongest advocate and one of his most trusted friends. All the while, she maintains contact with the other, wealthier Boston through her granddaughter Betty, who becomes a radical, and through other members of her family who remain conservative while humoring Cornelia's dedication to social justice.

The almost incredulous duality of Cornelia as both an ex-officio member of high society and an adopted member of the immigrant class parallels a significant duality in the plot. Although *Boston* is mostly about "Bart" Vanzetti and "Nick" Sacco, and the reader's emotions are engaged almost exclusively by their plight, the third person narration switches at times to another legal case—one involving the financial "murder" of a self-made industrialist by a clique of Boston financiers. Ironically, in this case (of Jerry Walker, which parallels an actual financial scandal in Boston[15]) the courts are eventually persuaded to overturn an initial ruling which had gone against the men of wealth and position. Sinclair's point here, of course, is that the law obeys the dollar and does in the Jerry Walker case what it claims it has no right to do in the Sacco-Vanzetti case.

Except for such digressions into high capitalism, or into the high society of Cornelia's rich relatives, the story focuses on the accused Italians. In the first two hundred pages, up to the arrest, Sinclair concentrates on detailing the personality and mind of Bart Vanzetti as Cornelia comes to know them. This section also describes both the

Boston police strike of 1919 and the Palmer Raids of 1920, two events indicating the reactionary political climate of the early twenties. Sinclair then presents the Bridgewater trial of Vanzetti and, in much greater detail, the controversial Dedham trial of both anarchists. Here the novelist follows the legal records except for the invention of Len Swenson as the first lawyer retained by the defense (and who unsuccessfully begs Cornelia to perjure herself for the sake of the defendants). Always willing to intervene rhetorically against the prosecution, the judge, and other officials who seem to prevent legal justice, Sinclair continues the story until the death and then the funeral of the two Italians. In the last two hundred and fifty pages, which cover the final, desperate four months of life for Vanzetti and Sacco, he conveys both a sense of martyrdom surrounding the defendants and a sense of helplessness on the part of such devoted and hard-working supporters as Cornelia Thornwell.

III   *Literary Achievement*

Aside from the fact that *Boston* is really too long and demands unusual persistence and perhaps even an initial sympathy for Sacco and Vanzetti, its weaknesses fall into four categories: rhetorical stance, structure, characterization, and content. Sinclair's relationship with his audience, the rhetorical stance of the novel, is typically didactic. As always, Sinclair wrote for the masses, and he seldom assumed that they wanted sophisticated fiction. Many times he intrudes into his narrative to point up his lessons—though this is not as bothersome in *Boston* as in many other novels. At the end of the novel, for instance, he does not let the reader draw his own conclusion about the significance of Sacco and Vanzetti. Rather, the reader is given Sinclair's Socialist slant: "To a hundred million groping, and ten times as many still in slumber, the names of Sacco and Vanzetti would be the eternal symbols of a dream, identical with civilization itself, of a human society in which wealth belongs to the producers of wealth, and the rewards of labor are given to the laborers" (754–55).

Flaws in structure and characterization seem more serious. The fact that the novel begins as the story of Cornelia, particularly in the first half of Volume I, and then becomes almost exclusively the story of the Sacco-Vanzetti case throughout the second volume is disturbing. The second volume is more unified, more to the point of the tragedy, and more serious than the first. The continual movement from the case of the two Italians to the upper reaches of Boston society, in both volumes, is also disturbing, although it provides a

radical understanding of the socio-economic context of the case.
Neither one of these weaknesses, though, is as damaging as Sinclair's
characterization of upper-class figures. Cornelia herself clings at
times to her convictions with an extraordinary, perhaps even
excessive, tenacity; and with the notable exception of her son-in-law
Henry Cabot Winters, her relatives often seem to be two-
dimensional cutouts, perfect Socialist silhouettes of the upper class.

Like *Oil!* the novel contains no obvious propagandizing, and is
remarkably objective in its presentation of the Sacco-Vanzetti case,
yet its content is shaped by a Socialistic bias. Occasionally, when
Sinclair describes immoral behavior among the rich in the novel, he
seems to be doing no more than leering. At other points he inserts
such definitions of capitalism as "the will of a predatory class" (658).
But the real impact of his Socialist posture can be seen in the analysis
of American society that emerges from *Boston*—an analysis which
stresses the oppression of the lower classes and the predatory
nature of the upper but which almost completely neglects the
existence of a middle class. Since the fears that made the prejudiced
trial of Sacco and Vanzetti possible were largely middle-class fears
of violence and alien radicalism, this is a serious omission.

The achievement of the novel, however, generally vitiates such
flaws. In the first place, the plot itself is rich with historical detail and
little known but important facts about the Sacco-Vanzetti case. The
Boston police strike, the Palmer Raids, the general public paranoia
concerning radicals in the early twenties, the continual disagree-
ment among radical factions during the defense efforts, the dis-
crepancies in the trial, the strange assortment of evidence and
witnesses for both the prosecution and the defense, the final legal
maneuvering involving higher courts and the Massachusetts governor, and the various demonstrations in Boston in 1927 are all woven
into the narrative of Cornelia Thornwell, Boston society, and Bart
Vanzetti. *Boston* is an excellent entrance into the tone and circumstances of radical politics throughout the decade of the twenties.

It is also a fairly objective presentation of the Sacco-Vanzetti case.
In his short preface to the novel Sinclair says, "I wish to make clear
that I have not written a brief for the Sacco-Vanzetti defense" (vi). In
spite of his depiction of the case as a tragic miscarriage of justice, and
his inclusion of many reasons for believing in Vanzetti's (though not
necessarily Sacco's) innocence,[16] his story is devoted largely to facts.
His omniscient persona never says that the two Italians are innocent;
through his heroine he avoids an approval of Vanzetti's anarchism; he

depicts the defense as willing at one point to engage in perjury; and
he rightly shows the defense—"a committee of anarchists was a
contradiction in terms" (496)—as factitious and at odds among
themselves. Perhaps the strongest evidence of a worthwhile objectivity in the novel occurs when Sinclair has Cornelia engage in a
discussion with her son-in-law over the philosophy of political
anarchism (454–63). Cornelia admits that she does not know Sacco
well enough to state that he is not an advocate of violence. When the
dialogue remains on the subject of anarchism, especially the
possibility of Vanzetti's belief in violence as a means to combat
oppression, Cornelia's son-in-law, Henry Cabot Winters, brings out
copies of anarchist propaganda that Vanzetti had distributed. Rather
than apologize or attempt to explain anarchism as essentially
nonviolent, Sinclair allows Winters to point out some obviously
disturbing facts, such as bomb diagrams in Vanzetti's pamphlets. This
scene allows Sinclair to convey an implicit disapproval of the
tendency towards violence in anarchism, as well as an understanding
of the nature of conditions in America that could push radicals to
violence. But he does not construe anarchism as innocuous.

While some characters are weak in the novel, others are developed
quite well. Henry Cabot Winters, for example, who is a wealthy
lawyer, is not the usual upper-class stereotype of Sinclair's fiction;
instead, he is a fallible human being who eventually shows traces of
sympathy for his mother-in-law's social conscience. Two agents of
injustice in the novel, Judge Webster Thayer and Governor Alvin T.
Fuller, are explained and described with remarkably little bitterness. But the character who is presented the most effectively is
Bartolomeo Vanzetti. For Sinclair a chief purpose in writing the
novel (as in *The Jungle*) was to offer an alternative to the usual image
of the immigrant, particularly the immigrant radical, as inexorably
different in some dirty, nefarious way from ordinary Americans. Just
as *The Jungle* was in part an attempt to identify honest, American
qualities in Lithuanian immigrants in Packingtown, *Boston* was an
attempt to convey the nobility of Vanzetti. Therefore, in Volume I
Sinclair continually stresses Vanzetti's social idealism, his love of
children and nature, his interest in Dante as well as in revolutionary
or anarchistic writers, and the strong personal convictions that are
the foundations of his political posture. Whenever possible Sinclair
uses Vanzetti's own published words, from letters and interviews, in
the dialogue. Since in real life Vanzetti was a man of unusual inner
strength, it is difficult to judge the extent to which Sinclair idealized

him in *Boston.* Towards the end of the novel, however, many statements about him have a ring of validity to them: "He was gentle, he was wise, and he was dignified. The humiliations of prison life had failed to affect him; he had conquered his jailers" (527).

As a result of the convincing presentation of Vanzetti as a noble, dignified, and intelligent human being, the novel achieves in its later chapters an eventual, compelling sense of desperation and doom mingled with bitterness and incredulity. Earlier parts of the story seem to be weakened by Sinclair's usual optimistic tone even in the face of serious and tragic events; the author appears to be having too much fun with his story to really be disturbed about the case. But the inexorability of death, as well as the strongly felt fact of injustice, permeate the last two hundred pages of *Boston.* In tone—a particularly deficient, or at least uneven, quality in many of Sinclair's novels—the second volume of *Boston* is as powerful as anything Sinclair wrote after *The Jungle.*

IV   *The Theme of Complicity*

Boston contains one obvious and intriguing departure from the facts of the Sacco-Vanzetti case. In reality the first lawyer hired by the Defense Committee was Fred Moore, a veteran of court battles involving labor leaders. But in the novel the first lawyer is named Len Swenson; and he is not meant to be a fictional representation of Moore, for Moore also appears later in the story. Sinclair creates Swenson so that he may have a member of the defense propose to Cornelia that she perjure herself. Swenson does ask her to do this—to state before the judge and jury of the original trial that she had been with Vanzetti on the day that the South Braintree murders occurred (364).

This fictitious proposal and its rejection by Cornelia—a purely academic and hypothetical event inserted into the factual narrative—is important because it introduces a univeral element into the facts of the case as they are presented in the novel. If Sinclair had only intended to publicize the case, only to write his "contemporary historical novel," there was little need for a fictitious defense attorney and even less need for that attorney to recommend perjury to Cornelia as a means to an honorable end. But Sinclair had more intentions than publicity and sympathy for Sacco and Vanzetti when he wrote the novel. He wished also to make a case for truth itself. In this thematic respect *Boston* is his most mature novel.

There are several ways in which Sinclair argues for truth in his story. He strongly criticizes the courtroom procedure of the prosecution and the judge as an attempt to smother the truth with deception and fear, and he suggests that the investigation of the case by Governor Fuller is geared to gather evidence to support the original conviction rather than to uncover the real facts. But Sinclair makes his most effective claim for the validity of truth by having Cornelia refuse to perjure herself. If she could do so, Swenson explains, Sacco and Vanzetti would be acquitted; for no one in the jury or among the prosecution would dare to challenge the word of an ex-governor's wife. In fact, since Cornelia is herself certain of Vanzetti's innocence and believes that his original alibi supported by witnesses from the Italian community is true, her perjury would not be a serious lie, perhaps not a lie at all. However, in spite of her certainty of the defendant's innocence and her admiration of him as a noble human being, she refuses to deceive the court in his behalf. Why?

Perhaps Sinclair intended only to create suspense or to suggest what might well have happened on occasion in 1921 as the defense found its efforts to present alibis hindered by the jury's refusal to accept and believe Italian witnesses. But another explanation for the Swenson proposal is suggested later in the story when Cornelia tells her children that "from first to last there has not been one honest man who had anything to do with it [the case] on the government side" (692). Obviously, then, her refusal to perjure herself is a means of morally staying out of the enemy's camp. For Cornelia, and by extension for Sinclair, morality itself is more important than politics, more important than making sure that Sacco and Vanzetti do not suffer needlessly because of legal injustice. Cornelia cannot fight the fire of deception and dishonesty with more dishonesty.

By having Cornelia reject Swenson's proposal that she perjure herself, Sinclair openly indicates that expediency—even if it is merciful and compassionate—is not reform, is not the proper response to injustice. In this manner he establishes a subtle theme of complicity in his novel. Complicity—involvement in deception and dishonesty—is what Cornelia avoids, in spite of her emotional and political ties with Vanzetti, and is what the prosecution, the judge, the governor, and the reactionary public do not avoid. *Boston* is more than a story of facts interestingly presented behind the mask of fiction; it is a sweeping indictment of all who refuse to understand the interdependency of man in society, of those who are blinded by selfish interests or by prejudice to the reasons behind Sacco and Vanzetti, and even of those who do not see the great injustice of some men profiting very much by the labor of those who hardly profit at all. The story pleads for truth, which is too often sacrificed to either selfishness or expediency, and for an understanding of the web of relationships—economic, social, and moral—which implicate most of America in the tragedy of Sacco and Vanzetti.

CHAPTER 9

The Thirties

$\mathbf{A}$FTER the achievement of *Boston* Sinclair's writings increased in volume. During the last three decades of his career he produced a total of forty-five books. These later writings seem in general to approach journalism rather than art and are somewhat less significant and less powerful than the works he generated during the first half of his career. Even from a political perspective his later years appear rather skewed, mainly because of his shifting posture: he was an independent Socialist in the late twenties and very early thirties, a liberal Democrat after 1933 but also an ardent defender of Stalin's policies even after the Moscow trials and purges of the late thirties (though he never became a member of the Communist Party), and a fairly obvious anti-Communist after World War II.[1] That Sinclair, in one year, could write about "My Long Love Affair" (with his wife Mary Craig) in *Personal Romances*, publish an anti-Catholic novel in which the mother of Jesus appears by psychic means at a Notre Dame football game,[2] and defend Stalin's terror against the assertions of a visitor recently returned from the U.S.S.R.[3] suggests the kind of contradictions which, while both present and visible in his earlier years, were especially noticeable from the thirties on.

The decade from 1929 through 1938, the sixth decade of his life, was certainly Sinclair's busiest. During these years he ran a close race for election as the governor of California, led a major political movement of the depression, and published nine novels and nine major books of nonfiction. By 1938 Upton Sinclair had made himself a permanent fixture in both literary and political life in America.

I The Middle of the Journey

The source of the contradictions that stalked Sinclair's thought were publicly revealed, in part, in 1932 when he published *American Outpost*, an autobiography which he enlarged in 1962 without much revision of earlier material. The manuscript was

124

actually drafted in 1929,[4] a fact which serves to explain its tone (by establishing that it was written before the stock market crash) and suggests a way of accounting for the mediocre novels he published in 1930 and 1931.

American Outpost presented Sinclair to his American audience as a kind of radical quite different from the image offered in many of his other works, especially the harsh economic determinist of his "Dead Hand" analyses. Many of the facts of his early life narrated in the autobiography have been mentioned in the early chapters of this study: his aristocratic Southern roots, his alcoholic father and overprotective mother, his early infatuation with religion and sexual moralism, the difficulties in his first marriage caused by his obsession with becoming a serious writer, his conversion to Socialism, the breakup of his first marriage and his next marriage to Mary Craig Kimbrough, his experimentations with diet reform and psychic phenomena as well as muckraking, and his problems of getting his work before the public. In opening up this information to the reading public, Sinclair was suggesting that his sensibility was that of a Romantic idealist rather than that of a Marxist social critic. The "outpost" referred to in the title of his book was one of personal rebellion against all the aspects of life—from liquor to sexual immorality to economic inequality—that offended his idealistic assumptions.

The autobiography also stressed Sinclair's Southern origins to a surprising degree. Sinclair was careful to indicate the Southern styles that he had eradicated in his own bearing: dependency on alcohol, defense of antebellum societal arrangements, and deference to the material comforts of affluence. But at times the book flaunts his respectable ancestors and suggests that Sinclair believed strongly in a genealogy of social position. As C. Hartley Grattan speculated in 1932, "his annoying attitude of didactically giving instruction to his readers about the meaning of social phenomena is an unconscious hangover of his feeling that he is just a little better than his readers."[5]

Grattan also commented on the candor of *American Outpost*, saying that Sinclair's snobbishness "detracts fatally from the charm of his work except in this book, where he hints at the genesis of the peculiarity. For essentially Sinclair is a charming man." The autobiographical honesty in the book—in which Sinclair even tells of the abnormal chastity he tried to practice in his first marriage—is its most admirable quality.

Its almost complete lack of bitterness and of "social protest" combined with touches of light humor make the autobiography something of an anomaly in Sinclair's career up to 1932. It is not easy to understand why Sinclair would engage in such lightheartedness immediately after the fatalistic narrative of *Boston*. One plausible reason is that beneath the facade of his rhetoric Sinclair was essentially a gentle, sometimes even nonchalant, person whose approach to experience was primarily that of genteel curiosity. This image of Sinclair suggests that he was not sufficiently *serious*—or not serious for sufficient periods of time—to satisfy the demands of hardboiled Marxian radicalism. That he could parade around the streets of Boston sandwiched between oversized fig leaves while gathering information on the tragedy of Sacco and Vanzetti is compelling support for such an impression. However, a more logical as well as generous interpretation would suggest that the lightheartedness, the nonchalance, the lack of seriousness, and facetiousness, the tendency towards fantasy in Sinclair, were all part of a defense system of a sensitive personality that had been extensively and painfully shocked by both personal and social reality. The clue to this interpretation, in the autobiography at least, is that Sinclair dwelt almost exclusively on the difficult years before his second marriage, covering the period after 1913 in only ten out of two hundred seventy pages.

American Outpost was primarily and most noticeably Sinclair's way of pausing to look back over the first five decades of his life, with extreme emphasis on the years of his first marriage. Having become a kind of public institution by the late twenties, Sinclair may also have intended to justify his idiosyncratic role to ready him for the years to come. Whatever its purpose, the writing of *American Outpost,* which Sinclair must have begun immediately after finishing *Boston,* serves as a convenient dividing line between the striving and often forceful products of his early career, and the somewhat less strident expressions of his later career.

II *Decline and Fall*

Sinclair's first published fruits after composing his autobiography were three misdirected novels and a book dealing with psychic phenomena, *Mental Radio* (1930). This last book was both an expression of Sinclair's open mindedness and a sign of his willingness to be sidetracked off the high road of social protest. *Mountain City* (1930), *Roman Holiday* (1931), and *The Wet Parade* (1931), the

novels, were signs of what might be called a failure of artistic nerve
after the accomplishments of *Oil!* and *Boston.*

Mountain City and *Roman Holiday* cannot really be called failures
of imagination as they are both ingeniously plotted—with *Roman
Holiday* incorporating the more clever story. In *Mountain City*
Sinclair reached back to his juvenile hack plots for a story of success
by a hard-working and scrupulously capitalistic young man, Jed
Rusher. "Mountain City" is Denver, and Sinclair claimed to have
patterned his protagonist after an actual resident of that city. In the
novel Rusher, obviously the vehicle for attempted satire, could also
be interpreted as leading the kind of life that Upton Sinclair might
have himself led if his young dreams of success had led him into the
realm of business rather than literature. Son of an alcoholic father,
Rusher early learns that money is the key to the fulfillment of life.
"Get money, Jed Rusher, get money" is his constant motivation
throughout a plot from which he emerges as a wealthy but cruel
financier. His final act in the story is to endow Mountain City College
with fifty thousand dollars for an academic chair to combat such
"economic fallacies" as Socialism and the Single Tax.

In *Roman Holiday* Sinclair once again indulged his penchant for
fantasy in a story which, for the first time in his career, featured the
conversion of a reactionary plutocrat to the gospel of social justice.
Unlike Hal Warner, Bunny Ross, or Cornelia Thornwell, the
protagonist of *Roman Holiday* is no right-hearted incipient idealist at
the beginning of the story. Rather, he is Luke Faber, the scion of a
wealthy New England family, who (quite unlike the cautious
stereotypical New England aristocrat) belongs to the American Legion
and advocates "direct action" mob politics against suspected radicals.
Luke Faber is also an amateur race car driver, and he has the
misfortune to be seriously injured in a racing accident. When he is
hospitalized his mind regresses psychically to the Roman Empire in
138 B.C. There he begins to realize that the forces at work in the
decline of the Empire are remarkably similar to the forces at work in
contemporary America. In particular, Faber sees that Roman
Legionnaires are used to brutally beat down plebeian strikers. During
this "Roman Holiday" Faber's girlfriend appears as a plebe and is
killed as a result of Legionnaire violence. When Faber regains
consciousness back in 1930 America, his previous reactionary
attitudes are reversed.

Mountain City and *Roman Holiday,* in spite of their plot virtues, are faulty as art and as expressions of a radical political posture. Sinclair created caricatures rather than characters. Jed Rusher and Luke Faber are simply *types* of persons. Neither protagonist suggests the inner dynamics of J. Arnold Ross in *Oil!* The problem of character is of course greater in satire than in any other fictional mode, and Sinclair, with his tendency to engage in absolute judgment of his characters based on their personal social philosophies, always had particular trouble with satire. *Mountain City* and *Roman Holiday* would have been better novels if Sinclair had chosen once again to explore the region of motivation and feeling in his capitalist characters—as in *Oil!* and as in Dreiser's *The Financier* and Lewis's *Babbitt*—rather than exploit them to make points that radicals needed no urging to accept and conservatives would automatically reject.

Even as political statements the two novels seem ambiguous at best. Why did Sinclair choose to deal primarily with the upper class in both novels? And where in either is a sense of an available collective answer—Socialism or even the mechanics of established politics—to the social and political problems raised? Previously, especially in the pages of *Money Writes!*, Sinclair had stated that "the ideals of revolutionary labor are identical with those of the vital creative artist."[6] In the thirties, furthermore, other American radical writers took inspiration from the Sacco-Vanzetti affair, using the two executed men as an "image of the working class and as the raw material of the new social order."[7] Ironically, in 1930 and 1931, as well as later in the decade, Sinclair wrote about the American plutocracy—critically, of course, but to the exclusion of the working class and antipathetic to the developing mode of proletarian fiction.

In *The Wet Parade* Sinclair drew his characters primarily from the working class but aimed his rhetoric at alcohol rather than class differences. Always a teetotaler and burdened with memories of his alcoholic father and of two heavy drinking literary friends, Jack London and George Sterling (both of whom had committed suicide), Sinclair began seriously thinking about a pro-prohibition novel in 1930 after the *Literary Digest* published the results of a poll that showed most Americans to be in favor of repealing the noble experiment. In a letter to the *New Republic* in August 1930 Sinclair attacked the accuracy of the *Digest* poll and said that less than one fourth of the states would vote for repeal of the Eighteenth Amendment. In addition to misreading American desires in such a gross fashion, Sinclair also threatened the kind of violence that he could never completely accept as a means of achieving economic equality, saying that if appeal ever became a serious possibility a squadron of "consecrated women" would shut down every speakeasy in New York City even if they faced brutality and physical injury from Tammany Hall gangsters in the process.[8]

Apparently as an attempt to insure that such Carrie Nations would not have to injure themselves storming the barricades, Sinclair wrote *The Wet Parade*. Perhaps more importantly, the novel also provided him with the means of using his New York childhood as the stuff of fiction. The story concerns two young adults, Maggie May Chilcote and Kip Tarleton, both of whom are projections of Sinclair himself, Southerners by birth and heritage, residents of New York City, and children of alcoholics. Maggie May's father is a suicide, and she is in New York to give whatever assistance she can to her brother, an alcoholic poet. Kip's father is an alcoholic who eventually dies in the family hotel managed by his mother. Much of the setting in the novel and all of the Chilcote and Tarleton relatives are obviously based on Sinclair's childhood recollections of the Weisinger House on West Nineteenth Street. As the story progresses Maggie May and Kip marry. After he loses one job because he refuses to cover up his rich employer's bootlegging, Kip becomes a prohibition agent who takes his responsibilities with the utmost seriousness. Meanwhile his wife becomes a temperance lecturer of no less enthusiasm. At the end of the novel Kip is murdered in the pursuit of his duties. In her final temperance lecture his wife advises women to be ready to attack saloons with their hatchets. Sinclair's closing words are:

> PROHIBITION HAS NOT FAILED!
> PROHIBITION HAS NOT BEEN TRIED!
> TRY IT!

The plot of *The Wet Parade* is thus completely rhetorical; nothing that happens in the story belies Sinclair's prohibition argument, and the overall tone of the novel is seriousness and sadness. Yet in spite of Sinclair's temperance zeal the story seems to emphasize the *difficulties* involved in prohibition more than its feasibility, and in fact to imply that the violence eventually urged by Mrs. Tarleton might become a necessity.

The Wet Parade is primarily a historical and biographical document. Its topical nature in 1931 encouraged Metro-Goldwyn-Mayer to turn it into a movie starring Robert Young and Jimmy Durante;

and its projection of Sinclair's attitudes towards his childhood and family makes it an essential book for any scholar interested in understanding its author. But like *Mountain City* and *Roman Holiday,* and in spite of its brooding seriousness—which the two previous novels lack—it cannot be called a work of art. In 1931 no reviewer made this point better than H. L. Mencken, friend of both Sinclair and the American saloon, and admirer of many of Sinclair's earlier novels:

> His cunning as a literary artist does not diminish. His dialogue is highly polished. "Please, please, Papa!" cries Maggie May to her wine-cursed father, Mr. Roger Chilcote. "Please do not drink any more!" "Oh, little girl, little girl," he replies, "what can Papa do? I cannot give it up! It is a fiend that has got me!" There are also some pretty passages between Maggie May's brother, Roger II, and his various loves. One of them is Miss Lilian Ashton, an actress. "No, Roger!" she exclaims, "I am not worthy of you! I have soiled myself." To which he replies genially: "I am no spring chicken myself, kid! Forget it!" "Such," observes Mr. Sinclair, "was romance made real." . . .
>
> Such stuff moves me, and I like a lot of it. "The Wet Parade" runs to 431 pages of small print, and is good value for the money. [9]

III *Epic*

After *The Wet Parade* Sinclair did not write another novel for five years. Instead, he became involved in electoral politics. Such involvement was motivated partly by opportunity, for Sinclair suddenly found his version of Socialism, once he became willing to subsume it within the California Democratic Party, acceptable as a response to the depression. His willingness to run for office seriously as the candidate of a major party (in the past he had run several times on the Socialist ticket, but such attempts had been mainly symbolic) may also have been related to less obvious factors. One possible reason was the temporary playing out of novelistic powers evident in his three works of 1930–1931. Another may have been a brief but powerful disenchantment with art itself caused by a disappointing financial affair with the Russian movie director Sergei Eisenstein in which Sinclair raised monetary support for *Que Viva Mexico* only to feel, eventually, that Eisenstein was making poor use of his support. Also, Sinclair was developing an increasing faith in the feasibility of class cooperation—rather than conflict—in American politics. The end result, whatever its causes, was the End Poverty in California, or EPIC, movement.

Two books published by Sinclair in 1933 demonstrate the changes in his political thought that prepared the way for his EPIC involvement. *Upton Sinclair Presents William Fox* was the presentation of the movie mogul's argument that in spite of his own past financial transgressions he was being unfairly persecuted by his creditors. Since Fox paid Sinclair to put his story down, Sinclair was only the medium for the argument. Yet he was privy to Fox's stated dream of making educational pictures inexpensively available to schools and churches, and he grew hopeful that a multimillionaire might even let his industry be nationalized.[10] Fox had no intention of such altruism, of course, but Sinclair was not seriously discouraged, for he next published *The Way Out*, a series of letters to a hypothetical industrialist named Perry and others like him: "captains and managers of industry, as well as professional people, doctors, lawyers, editors, writers."[11] Plainly written, Sinclair's letters indicate that the way out of the depression is through nationalization of industry followed by a policy of production for use rather than production for profit. The means of nationalization would be altruism on the part of the present owners of industry: "We propose," Sinclair says to Perry, "that you surrender your privileges as a profit-maker and accept in return your rights as a citizen of industry." "Is it altogether a Utopian dream," he continues, "that once in history a ruling class might be willing to make the great surrender, and permit social change to come about without hatred, turmoil, and waste of human life?"[12]

Sinclair's hopes were of course a Utopian dream; yet having expressed such eloquent optimism, he could hardly have turned down California Democrats when they asked him to consider entering the primary for governor in 1934. Sinclair agreed to do so, wrote a book entitled *I, Governor of California, and How I Ended Poverty* (1933), and found himself the leader of a state political movement with national prospects.

As this study is not a political biography, there is no need to deal at length here with Sinclair's EPIC movement except to indicate its nature and postulate its effect on his writing career. What Sinclair outlined in *I, Governor* was a plan to end poverty by putting the unemployed to work in state-owned industrial colonies supported by bonds of small denomination and by confiscatory taxation of banks, stock shares, high incomes, and inheritances. After Sinclair won the Democratic primary in August 1934, he changed his formula somewhat to "Immediate EPIC," dropping the idea of confiscatory taxes and obviously trying to appeal to middle and even upper-class voters. In the general election against Republican Frank Merriam, Sinclair was subjected to slander and misrepresentation at the hands of the mass media and political opponents, who dug diligently into his early writings to "prove" that he was a Communist, an opponent of the family, a free lover, or some other variety of dangerous radical. He lost the election to Merriam, wrote *I, Candidate for Governor and How I Got Licked* (1935), and devoted his EPIC organization (including a weekly journal) to persuading the national Democratic party to adopt a "production for use" philosophy. Although EPIC was not able to significantly shape the Democratic platform in 1936 (one of Sinclair's practical hopes, as Arthur M. Schlesinger, Jr has pointed out) EPIC was an important factor in the leftward trend of Roosevelt's second term in office. [13]

The effects of Sinclair's EPIC experience on his later writing were numerous. In the first place, after his contact with political realities, Sinclair was never again to be quite the rhetorical radical he was before 1930, except in his rigid defense of Stalin in the late thirties, and he was never again to write compellingly in fiction of the proletariat as he had in *The Jungle* and *Boston*. He was, instead, to move his stories increasingly through the lives of the upper classes or, as in the Lanny Budd novels, through the important events and around the important figures of history. Nor was he ever to write fiction quite as seriously as he had before EPIC; the tone of much of his later work, even the Lanny Budd series, is distinctly and sometimes disturbingly lighthearted. Sinclair's lack of tangible success in practical politics—especially as a result of the vicious campaign waged against him in California—would very easily have made another man bitter, disillusioned, cynical. But Sinclair's optimism was strangely invincible, and political disappointment apparently served only to convince him that his primary calling was literature.

IV   A Return to Fiction

From 1935 to 1962 Sinclair published only three or four major nonfiction books. The rest were novels or plays. The first work of Sinclair's post-EPIC career was in fact a direct product of it, a 1936 novel entitled *Co-Op* and presenting the case for government-supported cooperatives on the order of the industrial colonies that formed the heart of the original EPIC plans. Primarily, in the context of 1936 and the growing uneasiness of many liberals over the apparent ineffectiveness of many New Deal programs, *Co-Op* was an examination of one possible way to alleviate depression conditions. As such it was couched in a rather nonpartisan perspective—neither Democratic, Socialist, nor Communist—although Sinclair's social analysis was, as usual, anticapitalist. Implied within its pages was a gentle criticism of the eclectic and often blind domestic policies of Roosevelt's first term.

The plot of the novel revolves around the growth of the fictional San Sebastian (probably Long Beach) Self-Help Exchange. The Exchange is a cooperative organization of the unemployed for the purpose of production and barter. It is begun by several men who at the beginning of the novel live in a "Hooverville"; these leaders of the cooperative are Charlie Day, an ex-publicity man, and Sig Soren, a Dane who after a youthful career of vagabondage has become very interested in cooperatives as a means of gradually achieving national economic equality. Over eighty characters appear in the story of the co-op as it develops, ranging from the poorest unemployed, who are desperate enough even to concoct a stew out of their pet dog, to the richest capitalists of San Sebastian, who build fortifications against an impending revolution of the proletariat. The central figure, though, is Sig Soren. His nonpartisan belief in co-ops as a gradual and inoffensive (to capitalists) means for the working class to gain the tools of production is the political logic of the novel. For the sake of plot interest Sinclair includes two love affairs: one between Soren and Maisie Trent, a well to do young woman who joins the co-op, and another between Mabel Saugus, a newly rich woman who supports the co-op financially, and Herbert Alding, a New Deal bureaucrat who eventually grows skeptical of bureaucracy. As the story progresses the San Sebastian Self-Help Exchange carefully avoids politics, wins the favor of a number of rich capitalists because of its goal of avoiding the "dole" by making the unemployed productive and self-sustaining, and grows in membership and effectiveness until the W.P.A. restricts its operations by assigning its best members to non-productive labor and by threatening to terminate government grants if the co-op begins to sell its products on the open market. Faced with this bureaucratic stupidity, Sig Soren travels to Washington where he is finally able to present the co-op's case to Roosevelt, who agrees to consider it. The future of the co-op at the close of the novel is uncertain.[14]

An attempt to publicize rather than to deliver a polemic, *Co-Op* resembles *Boston* in its basic intentions. Like the story of Sacco and Vanzetti, it is also highly objective. Sinclair portrays some millionaires as morally corrupted by their wealth, but he shows a surprising sympathy for many of them—especially for Theophilus Fleming, a self-made utilities baron. This compassion was probably generated by Sinclair's interest in seemingly social-minded plutocrats like William Fox and others he had come to know in Southern California. The one capitalist villain in the novel suffers from obvious paranoia and, Sinclair suggests, is an isolated case. Furthermore, the leaders of the co-op scrupulously avoid distinctly anticapitalist or antibusiness rhetoric; and they follow the soundest of business principles themselves, adapting where necessary to the established way of getting things done. Sinclair's growing political mildness, an allegiance to nonviolent, nonrevolutionary, and cooperative though leftish politics, is apparent throughout his story, which reflects the 1934 EPIC coalition of Socialists and Democrats.

Although it includes the usual collection of Sinclair's literary inabilities—jarring coincidences of plot, stereotyped characters with transparent motivations, and glib diction in both description and dialogue—the novel effectively presents some of the basic contradictions of the Great Depression. Due to Sinclair's own optimism, it does not convey the sense of human tragedy that Steinbeck's *The Grapes of Wrath* does. Even the suicide of a major character seems more like a mere event than a reason for sadness. Yet, Sinclair succeeds in sketching the following contrasts in perceptive chiaroscuro: scenes of unemployment in conjunction with the hopes of the unemployed; the bureaucratic tangle of the New Deal and Roosevelt's open mindedness; the political paranoia of the wealthy right in conjunction with the disruptive mass action techniques of the Communists; and the possibility of economic solutions in conjunction with a basic American resistance to innovation.

Thematically, *Co-Op* only suggests the problem of the individual in society that informs many earlier novels. One reason for this limitation is Sinclair's decision not to depict any character *alone*. All of Sinclair's people seem to lead strictly social lives; they never brood in private. Actually, this feature had been salient in Sinclair's fiction ever since *Love's Pilgrimage*, except for a few observations about the inner problems of Bunny Ross and Cornelia Thornwell in *Oil!* and *Boston*. In *Co-Op* an inchoate tension between the individual and social forces is vitiated rather than explored by the communitarian ethos of the San Sebastian Self-Help Exchange (an extension, of sorts, of the Helicon Hall colony) and by the feigned absence of serious personal conflicts within the co-op.

V *Exploring the Plutocracy*

Sinclair's literary interests roamed picaresquely in 1936. Besides *Co-Op* he also published a fanciful children's story, *The Gnomobile: A Gnice Gnew Gnarrative with Gnonsense but Gnothing Gnaughty* (made into a Walt Disney movie in 1966), and an exposition of his "working religion," *What God Means to Me*. These two works reveal the two other aspects of Sinclair's personality: the lighthearted entertainer and the mystic. His religious treatise, defining his faith as positive and practical, lacking in a sense of original sin but supported and verified by his strange "ecstasies," is a particularly curious and revealing document. With the completion of these two expressions, Sinclair could return in 1937 and 1938 to the major concerns of *Mountain City, Roman Holiday*, and *The Way Out*: the nature of the American plutocracy and the possibility of its conversion to idealism.

Sinclair explored the plutocracy in three novels. The first, in 1937, was *The Flivver King*, a narrative interpretation of Henry Ford strung loosely on a plot involving the fortunes of both Ford and a family of Ford workers. Later in 1937 he published *No Pasaran!*, subtitled "A Story of the Battle of Madrid" and concerning a wealthy young man who gives up the life of high society in order to fight on the loyalist side in the Spanish Civil War. In 1938 Sinclair's major book was *Little Steel*, the story of a hesitant industrialist who refuses to take repressive measures against labor in spite of the advice of corrupt industrial counseling experts. Each of these three novels incorporates a liberal posture, but none effectively portrays the lower or working classes.

The Flivver King, demonstrating Sinclair's increasing affection for the United Auto Workers and other elements of the established labor movement, concentrates primarily on the inconsistencies in Ford's employee policies; in particular it points out his shift from the humaneness of his early years to his more oppressive later tactics (particularly his refusal to allow unions in his plants). Sinclair argues that Ford has become increasingly chained to the corrupting power of money because he "remained what he had been born; a super-mechanic with the mind of a stupid peasant."[15] The novel, like *Boston* but lacking its power, was another attempt to make undisguised history into fiction by merely adding fictional touches, in this case the parallel and unhappy story of the Shutt family which is interspersed between chapters dealing with Ford.

No Pasaran! ("They Shall Not Pass") was a reworking of the thematic problems of *Oil!* both in a new context—the Spanish Civil

War—and in the style of Sinclair's earliest juvenile writing. At first
Rudy Messer, a rich Columbia University student, is torn between
love for his reactionary family and friendship with a young Jewish
Socialist. The conflict, however, is rather easily resolved because the
liberal attraction is obviously noble while his family's attitudes are
obviously evil; at no time does the tension within Rudy Messer
approach the credibility of the tension within Bunny Ross. In fact,
Sinclair admits that his protagonist is really torn between "the powers
of heaven and hell contending."[16] After the powers of heaven are
victorious over his soul he and other "young American heroes"
victoriously hold off the Fascists at Madrid. Written in a hurry, *No
Pasaran!* reads like Sinclair's much earlier adventures of Mark
Malory or Clif Faraday, the cadet heroes of his juvenile work for
Street and Smith. For instance, in an adventuristic manipulation of
plot, Rudy's reactionary cousin ends up dead as the pilot of a Fascist
plane which is shot down at Madrid. But what may be more
disturbing in the story, in view of Sinclair's earlier admiration of the
working class, is the implication that the world is to be saved from
Fascism and capitalism primarily by aristocrats like Rudy Messer,
"the wonderful Rudy Messer"—as Sinclair has Rudy's dying Jewish
friend think of him (93).

The protagonist of *Little Steel* is an older aristocrat, Walter Judson
Quayle, head of Valleyville Steel Company and nominal head of his
traditional family. When a conspiracy of "Little Steel," an organization of independent steel companies determined to keep unions out
of their industry, tries to force him to sell out, Quayle resists and
begins to listen to the ideas of his daughter, wife of a young Socialist,
as well as those of Clum Jinkens, a technological wizard who calls
himself "Mr. Fixit" and travels around the country in "Susie," his
amazing self-contained motor home.[17] Although the possibility of
complexities, arising from Quayle's divided sense of responsibility to
his business, conservative family, and his radical daughter is
abundantly present, Sinclair never makes his protagonist's problems
seem sufficiently serious. The resulting story is jejune, relying too
strongly on conspiracy for complication (in the same manner that *No
Pasaran!* relies on a Fascist conspiracy), attempting to squeeze
novelty out of Mr. Fixit and his "house car," and avoiding any
significant treatment of the workers who stand to lose if Little Steel is
successful.

All three of these minor pieces of fiction provide evidence of a shift
in the direction of Sinclair's novelistic interests. In 1937 and 1938 he

was obviously moving away from the common man—particularly of lower-class origins—and towards characters who belong to a social, financial, or historical elite. He moved further in this direction immediately after *Little Steel*, writing about two famous women—the Virgin Mary and Marie Antoinette—in two separate works and then, in eleven volumes, sending the affluent Lanny Budd out to observe all the important events and figures of world history since 1913.

CHAPTER 10

The Triumph of Homiletic History

IN most of his writings Sinclair had functioned as one kind of historian or another. Only in *Manassas* did he appear as a true historical novelist, yet in much of his other work— fiction as well as nonfiction—he wrote both as a muckraking journalist presenting the ugly facts of recent events and as a visionary Socialist developing blueprints for the future based upon the unpleasant data of the past. In his novels, including even those that involve fantasy (such as *The Millennium*), Sinclair generally based his main characters on people he had met or read about. He was forever "putting people in," and he was often certain to indicate somewhere in his novel or else shortly afterwards in public statements that his characters were dramatizations of real life personalities. Unfortunately, in his less successful stories and to some extent in all of his fiction he relied too faithfully on his assumption that true to life facts about such people equaled effective characterization, forgetting that fiction demands the perception of human experience through emotion and empathy, not merely facts.

Between 1940 and 1949, falling back to his techniques in *Manassas,* Sinclair wrote ten long historical novels—one each year—tracing the history of the world from 1913 to 1946. The most remarkable, if not incredulous, feature of this series was that each novel takes as its central character a remarkable globetrotting American, Lanny Budd, the illegitimate son of a rich Connecticut munitions maker and a beautiful artist's model. In the Lanny Budd novels few significant historical events occur outside the presence of Lanny; like the earlier prototype Allan Montague of *Manassas,* Lanny simply goes everywhere and meets everyone of any historical importance. In *O Shepherd, Speak* in 1949, after Lanny had appeared as an agent of history from 1913 to 1946, making friends in the process with world leaders as diverse as Woodrow Wilson and Chairman Mao, Sinclair brought an apparent end to the fictional saga of Lanny Budd.

138

However, with the rise of a new threat to world peace in the form of global Communism (no longer a source of admiration for Sinclair), he published an eleventh and final volume, *The Return of Lanny Budd,* in 1953.

The Lanny Budd novels constitute a literary monument on the order of Mount Rushmore. As art they are mostly without virtue, but as works of great length, perserverance, spirit, and public approval, they cannot be ignored. The novels provided a decade of droll reviews by critics who found them implausible as fiction, but Sinclair readily admitted that he had no expectations of satisfying highbrow readers, and for the first time in his career since *The Jungle* his intuition and particular abilities uncovered a wide popular audience. Issued by the established Viking Press, the Lanny Budd novels sold over a million and a half copies in America alone; they also sold extensively in England and were translated into foreign editions in twenty other countries. *Dragon's Teeth* (1942), the third novel in the series, won the Pulitzer Prize for fiction, the only major award ever won by a Sinclair book. Probably, the most important aspect of the series is the gentle idealism that prevades the narratives: the continual hope for democratic Socialism, the obvious patriotism in the novels after 1941, the love for mankind and human nature that Sinclair persisted in demonstrating even while detailing the horrors of Hitler's Germany.

These facts suggest the difficulty of treating the Lanny Budd novels in a critical study. The easiest and perhaps the most appealing approach is to ridicule their weaknesses by echoing Sinclair's more intelligent reviewers. It is difficult to appreciate the novels as they were appreciated by popular readers and less demanding critics in the turbulent war days of the 1940's. Perhaps it is best to simply view the novels within the context of Sinclair's career—as a culmination of many aspects of his literary efforts, but not as his best work—while taking note of their more obvious faults and the reasons for their appeal.

I *World's End*

In 1938 and 1939 Sinclair reached far back into the past for two stories which, in his handling of them, were finger exercises for the full historical concert he began in 1940. In *Our Lady,* a fantasy about the mother of Jesus, and *Marie Antoinette,* a long and unproduced play, Sinclair indulged his historical curiosity concerning two famous and quite different women. The results of his curiosity are inferior to most of his earlier writing but are, nevertheless, instructive and revealing. *Our Lady* is an attack on Roman Catholicism which makes that faith's notion of the Virgin Mary the butt of a psychic joke. In the novel Mary, through the aid of a Galilean sorceress, appears at a Notre Dame University football game, where she astounds Catholic priests by revealing that she was most definitely not a virgin when her famous son was born.[1]

Both the facile narrative shifting (Galilee to Southern California, first century to twentieth) and the simplistic psychology of *Our Lady* reappeared in the Lanny Budd series. But the use of history in *Marie Antoinette* was a closer approximation to the turn that Sinclair's fiction was soon to take. In his play he tried to avoid obvious propaganda yet suggest his political idealism (in his case by using a chorus of voices chanting the slogans of the American and French Revolutions); and he also attempted to document a long important historical period (from Marie's first appearance in France to her death) through the private life and loves of a person intimately involved in the history of the period. *Marie Antoinette* was thus an attempt, however unsuccessful, at revealing history by means of an "inside narrative." By the next year, Sinclair had sharpened his technique and discovered that it was a mistake to work outside his own period of history.

The first Lanny Budd novel was *World's End*, and in writing it Sinclair at first had no intentions of carrying his story beyond 1919.[2] He was motivated by the direction history seemed to have taken in the late 1930's; in particular, he was obsessed with a fear of Fascism. His rigid anti-Fascist posture had even encouraged him to defend Stalin at a time when many American liberals had been disillusioned by terrorism and purges within the Soviet Union. In *Terror in Russia?*, a 1938 publication of letters between Sinclair and Eugene Lyons, a journalist and observer inside Russia for several years, Sinclair illogically excused Stalin's domestic policies as justified defenses against Fascist conspirators. This absolute detestation of Fascism understandably gave Sinclair a sense of historical regret for the unsatisfactory peace settlement following World War I, which he felt prepared the way for the dictatorships of Hitler, Mussolini, and Franco. As he explained when *World's End* was published in 1940, this sense of historical regret led to Lanny Budd. For his entire career, he said, he had been concerned primarily with American problems. "But all the time I was watching world events and hearing stories, and I suppose that whoever or whatever it is that works in the subconscious mind of a novelist was having his or her or its way with me; the big theme was stalking me and was bound to catch up. I saw the rise of Mussolini, and of Hitler, and of Franco; the dreadful agony of Spain wrung my heart; then I saw Munich, and said to myself, 'This is the end; the end of our world'."[3]

This explanation, written for a book club bulletin, identifies two key elements in the Lanny Budd novels. One is Sinclair's use of disturbing events, historical developments which "wrung [his] heart" and made him think that the doom of Western civilization was at hand. The other element is Sinclair's transcendent point of view, his assumption that not even impending doom could dampen his genius. His facetious statement about the "whoever or whatever" in his mind and the "big theme" that was "stalking" him suggests the ebullient spirit in which he could write of momentous and often tragic events. His playful use of words here indicates that Sinclair still had an optimistic outlook, even if "world's end" seemed apparent.

Even the act of writing *World's End* (and presumably the rest of the Lanny Budd novels) was a matter of creative enjoyment and "ecstasy" rather than somber reflection. "I was walking up and down in my garden one night, and something happened; a spring was touched, a button pressed—anyhow, a novel came rolling into the field of my mental vision; a whole series of events with the emotions that accompanied them, a string of characters, good and bad, old and young, rich and poor. I have had that happen to me before, but never with such force, such mass and persistence."[4] Sinclair suggested that this process might be described as "controlled multiple personality."

Given Sinclair's method of imagining his fiction, and realizing the length of his Lanny Budd novels (set in small wartime print, the shortest of the first ten books is nearly six hundred pages, and the longest is eight hundred fifty), it would be easy to assume that they were transcribed without much revision immediately from Sinclair's reveries. An important fact to understand, however, is that Sinclair probably spent more time per word on the series than on anything else he wrote. Unlike previous decades, the forties were free from other obligations, and he attempted little work besides his novels. His method was to write outdoors in the mornings and to revise his work at night. "This," he said, "is the ideal life for the writer. Sticking to it, day in and day out, rarely seeing anybody or going anywhere. . . . It is the hardest kind of work, yet also the most delightful play." His usual daily production, he said, was only a thousand words.[5] Furthermore, as he wrote he did extensive reading to collect information, and he sent his manuscripts to various persons to have them verify his facts.

In spite of the prize won by *Dragon's Teeth* and the greater popularity of *A World to Win* (which sold over seven hundred thousand copies in 1946), the first product of Sinclair's efforts is possibly the best. *World's End* tells the story of Lanny Budd from 1913 to 1919 as he grows from a hopeful, idealistic youth into a somewhat troubled observer of the world. Lanny is thirteen when the story begins; he has spent all his life in Europe where he lives with his mother Beauty Budd, who has been divorced for years from his industrialist father and is now a follower of the cosmopolitan pleasures available to great wealth. Significantly, the opening chapters reveal Lanny as a lover of art, of music and dancing, and an admirer of George Bernard Shaw. He is soon drawn into history by the advent of the Great War, and travels to America with his practical capitalist father Robbie Budd. Luckily, he finds himself included at the Versailles Peace Conference as a secretary to a Wilson aide, and is finally privy to the building conflict between capitalism and Socialist revolution after the success of the Bolsheviks in Russia. Not only is Lanny everywhere, but he also meets everybody—from Shaw to Lincoln Steffens, from Wilson to Sir Basil Zaharoff.

As history, *World's End*, like its ten followers, is both journalistic and encyclopedic. Nothing is really left out, and Sinclair devotes nearly three hundred pages to the Peace Conference alone. For the historical purposes of the novel, Lanny functions primarily as a lens, becoming Sinclair's way of probing newsreel-fashion into the making of the recent past. When Lanny is on the way to Paris, having attracted the attention of Professor Charles T. Alston, a Wilson adviser, Sinclair defines his hero's technical role. "The curtain was about to rise upon the last act of the great world melodrama which Lanny Budd had been watching through four and a half impressionable years. During the eight days of the steamer voyage his new friend helped him to peep through the curtain and see the leading characters taking their positions."[6]

In *World's End*, perhaps to a slightly larger degree than in most of the other novels, Lanny is more than a mere Peeping Tom looking curiously behind the curtains of history. The thematic burden he bears is blatantly indicated in the final scene of the novel when his father and Jessie Blackless, Lanny's radical uncle, indulge in an argument which Sinclair calls "The Battle of the Stags." To the nineteen year old Lanny,

This raging argument . . . became to him a symbol of the world in which he would have to live the rest of his life. His Uncle was the uplifted fist of the workers, clenched in deadly menace. As for Robbie, he had proclaimed himself the man behind the machine gun; the man who made it, and was ready to use it, personally, if need be, to mow down the clenched uplifted fists! As for Lanny, he didn't have to be any symbol, he was what he was, the man who loved art and beauty, reason and fair play, and pleaded for these things and got brushed aside. (737)

As Lanny's adventures continued after 1919 in the succeeding novels, and particularly after he transformed his love of reason and fair play into nonviolent democratic Socialism, he did become a symbol. Lanny Budd is Sinclair's overextended metaphor for the nineteenth century sensibility forced to exist in the troubled modern world. "It wasn't his world! It had no use for him!" (737) Lanny thinks in *World's End*; and even when Sinclair's fictional world finds a use for him as spy, diplomat, confidant of dictators, and presidential agent, his idealistic sensibility is still somehow at odds with events and necessities—his evocation of democratic Socialism is a hopeful and often heard, but not heeded voice.

Many earlier Sinclair protagonists—Jurgis Rudkus to some extent, the two Allan Montagues, Hal Warner, Bunny Ross, and Cornelia Thornwell—had filled a similar thematic role; but none had been quite so explicitly tormented by the raw forces of history itself. Although Lanny's divisions are represented by members of his family—not only by his father and his uncle but also his artistically inclined mother—the emotions he is caught up in most of the time are caused by and are directed at history. The narration of his episodes throughout the years thus suggests the interplay of Sinclair's own pre-modernist values and hopes with his realization—but not outspoken admission—of their potential ineffectiveness in the turmoil of the twentieth century. For this reason, in part, interpersonal relationships in *World's End* and the later novels are simply stand-ins for the drama of memory, hope, and regret that is carried on between Upton Sinclair and History. Even Lanny's love affairs—and there are several—tend to be rhetorical flourishes demonstrating historical circumstances or options.

II *World's Continuance*

Even though *World's End* pins the failure of the Paris Peace Conference on Sir Basil Zaharoff, the Russian-born British financier and munitions contractor, by showing his manipulation of Lloyd

George and Georges Clemenceau in particular, Sinclair obviously intended his story to be an anti-war novel. Perhaps partly motivated by a sense of guilt over his support of Wilson from 1917 to 1919, he suggests that international war offers capitalists a field day for profit taking and conspiratorial arrangements. In the novels written after 1940, Sinclair changed his objectives and became less the Socialist opponent of war and more the muckraker of world Fascism.

For convenience, the following chart lists all of the Lanny Budd novels and briefly indicates the periods of history covered in each:

I. *World's End* (published June 1940). The years 1913 to 1919.

II. *Between Two Worlds* (March 1941). The years 1920 to 1930, documenting in particular the rise of Fascism in Italy and Germany but suggesting that a similar trend was building in the United States until the stock market crash.

III. *Dragon's Teeth* (January 1942). The years 1930 to 1934, concentrating almost exclusively on events in Germany up to Hitler's Blood Purge.

IV. *Wide Is the Gate* (January 1943). The years 1934 to 1937, dealing with the beginnings of the Spanish Civil War in particular.

V. *Presidential Agent* (June 1944). The years 1937 and 1938, climaxing with the annexation of Austria, the Munich pact, and the invasion of Czechoslovakia, during which Lanny serves as a special agent for President Roosevelt.

VI. *Dragon Harvest* (June 1945). The years 1939 and 1940, between Franco's victory in Spain and the fall of France.

VII. *A World to Win* (May 1946). The years 1940 to 1942, up to America's entrance into the war.

VIII. *Presidential Mission* (May 1947). The years 1942 and 1943, especially concerning internal affairs in Germany, but also dealing with the progress of the war.

IX. *One Clear Call* (August 1948). The years 1943 and 1944, involving military manuevers in Europe and the possibility of advanced atomic technology in Germany.

X. *O Shepherd, Speak* (July 1949). From November 1944 to the summer of 1946.

XI. *The Return of Lanny Budd* (April 1953). From 1944 to 1949, the beginnings of the Cold War.

One can best summarize Sinclair's historical narratives by saying that they include about everything presented on the front page of *The New York Times* for nearly forty years. All events are unified by the adventures of Lanny as he observes and participates in them, eventually as a personal agent of Roosevelt and then of Truman. Throughout his encounters with history Lanny remains a devotee of reason and fair play, although he is converted to democratic Socialism during the 1920's and remains so thereafter, finally using his wealth for such purposes as a Peace Foundation (in *O Shepherd, Speak*) and the Free University of Berlin. In his personal life Lanny is something of an international playboy, particularly at first as he acts out his ostensible role as an art critic and dealer. His first two marriages, with women of incompatible social philosophies, end in divorce; but at the beginning of World War II (in *A World to Win*) he finally finds a permanent mate who is a spiritualist.

In addition to the incredulous ways in which Sinclair weaves Lanny Budd into the fabric of events, two other aspects of historiography in the series need to be emphasized. The first is Sinclair's conceptualization of history as conspiracy; the other is his growing patriotism, and lessening of anticapitalist fervor, throughout the last seven or eight volumes. Both the sense of conspiratorial forces and Sinclair's newfound nationalism demonstrate his intense anti-fascist posture throughout the forties.

Conspiracy pervades the world of Lanny Budd. Before, during, and immediately after World War I, the conspirators are Zaharoff, Rothschild, and other European industrial plutocrats. In the twenties these same men seem always to be manipulating events in Europe, while a similar small number of Wall Street bankers determine the political and economic atmosphere in the United States. The one nation which seems free of conspiratorial designs in the early novels is Russia. Most surprisingly, Sinclair asserts that capitalist conspirators have worked for both Mussolini and Hitler. Mussolini's ascendency in Italy is in fact partly prompted by a promise of financial backing from the House of Morgan, and Hitler in the early thirties seizes power essentially as the agent of industrial magnates in Germany. Later, Sinclair's history suggests that even in the United States Fascist plots (managed by such as Henry Ford, Charles Lindbergh, and Father Coughlin) are directed at President Roosevelt. Finally, after Yalta and the end of the war, the basic historical tension is the struggle of America against a worldwide, monolithic Communist conspiracy in favor of further war and subjugation.[7]

The adventures of Lanny take on patriotic overtones after the first four volumes. The reasons for this change are obvious: Sinclair's admiration for Roosevelt increased while his faith in the Russian Socialist experiment diminished. In *Presidential Agent* Lanny becomes precisely that after he meets F.D.R.; in this and later volumes

Lanny even assists Roosevelt in determining American foreign policy by writing several of his most important speeches. The most admirable quality of Roosevelt, Lanny feels, is his basic commitment to democratic Socialism in spite of his political realism and his need to pacify Roman Catholic and Southern supporters. At the end of the first novel featuring Roosevelt, Sinclair makes overwhelmingly clear his lack of detachment in using the President for the purposes of historical fiction. In pondering his association with both Hitler and Roosevelt, Lanny realizes that the world is torn by

a duel of wills between these two: one the champion of democracy, of government by popular consent, of the rights of the individual to think his own thoughts, to speak his own mind, to live his own life so long as he did not interfere with the equal rights of his fellows; the other the champion of those ancient dark forces of tyranny and oppression which had ruled the world before the concept of freedom had been born. . . .

Roosevelt versus Hitler! These two had not created the forces, but led them and embodied them. . . .[8]

In the first Lanny Budd novel the protagonist and antagonist of history had been Socialism and capitalism; in 1944, for Sinclair, the conflict of "forces" remained essentially the same, for Roosevelt embodied the spirit if not the letter of Socialist values, and Hitler was motivated by both capitalist values and capitalist individuals. Yet symbols of the conflict had changed and clarified. It was the tradition of freedom in America against the social philosophy of the Dark Ages which was still alive in Germany. Although Sinclair provided a scheme for understanding Hitler as something other than pure evil—as both an agent determined by historical forces and a determining force himself—the images in the novels published from 1942 to 1945 define Sinclair's rhetoric as pro-war propaganda. By 1953 Sinclair had even grown certain, within his obviously Manichean perspective, that American freedom was further threatened by once favored Communism—a certainty which motivates Lanny to turn in his half-sister to the F.B.I. as a Communist agent in *The Return of Lanny Budd.*

III *Public Appeal*

The Lanny Budd novels brought Sinclair the kind of popularity he desired but had not really achieved since 1906. His work was not a critical success, but even those reviewers of Lanny's adventures who found Sinclair's lack of literary finesse unpalatable were careful to praise his spirit and historical comprehensiveness. Some, like Maxwell Geismar, were even obliged to admit "that after you have accepted the complete absurdity of Mr. Sinclair's narrative . . . you begin to enjoy it."[9] The general reading public as well as less demanding reviewers were not even particularly dismayed by the absurdities. Sinclair's techniques and content won the generous approval of the public.

The Lanny Budd novels represent highly simplified history. Lanny himself, reviewers were quick to point out, resembles the comic book Superman in his marvelous appearances at all the right historical moments, and Sinclair's whole narrative might easily have been translated into several decades' worth of comic strip material. The way in which Sinclair allowed his readers to peer over the shoulders and into the private lives of important public figures was one factor which made the novels interesting for the general public.

The ideology behind the novels was probably the most publicly satisfying means of *morally* simplifying a tremendously complex period of history. In particular, Sinclair couched his stories in terms of grand historical forces: the force of progress, whether it was Communism in the 1920's or American democracy in the 1940's; and the force of oppression stemming from the distant past. Sinclair's suggestion that the progressive voice of freedom could eventually overwhelm the powers of reaction and greed in America was in effect a plea for readership. As Geismar noted in 1948, the Americans in the later volumes of Sinclair's series, in spite of their wealth and often careless power, "remain also generous and decent people who only want to establish prosperity and peace." Sinclair therefore expresses a "central view of life, which corresponds to our own earlier dreams of national destiny and to the Europeans' wildest fantasy."[10]

In addition to a Manichean dichotomy of historical forces, progressive and repressive, good and evil, the Lanny Budd novels also incorporate a perspective which is both Romantic and elitist. The prime movers, the agents of history, are the plutocrats, the aristocrats, the celebrated national leaders—never the masses or the common man. Furthermore, Sinclair's narrative seems to celebrate rather than condemn this basic fact about the development of twentieth century history. Lanny Budd himself is definitely elitist as well as American, both in his origins and his lifestyle. This emphasis on the *un*common man, a typical feature of sentimental historical fiction, accounts perhaps more than anything else for Sinclair's appeal to a readership which one scholar has postulated as "the restless, movie-minded, wealth-and-power envying, best-seller buying, and world-event following audience."[11]

This brand of elitism in the Lanny Budd novels may be seen as damaging or restricting to the resulting point of view. Sinclair's choice of a member of the American upper class as his central consciousness puts serious limits on both characterization and historical perception. Lanny—like the two Allan Montagues in *Manassas, The Metropolis,* and *The Moneychangers*—appears projected into history by a power similar to wish fulfillment. This point need not be overemphasized, but Lanny Budd may well act as Upton Sinclair's alter ego—his playfully exaggerated construction of what he possibly would have chosen to be if he had had such a choice.

It is easy to admire the basic thought processes behind these novels by recognizing that they represent both Sinclair's willing acceptance of the world as it is, and as it has been made, and his hopeful demand for its reformation. In a humane paradox, Sinclair seems to cherish the world of Lanny Budd that he describes so verbosely, even to express a kind of literary or historical love for it as he develops his lengthy expositions of events and forces. Yet, he also pleads for democratic Socialism as a means of achieving a reliable future.

It is important to point out that the elitist world which Sinclair accepts as worthy of his efforts is not necessarily the world that everyone would accept. It is a world highly managed by powerful leaders, heroic personalities and arch villains; and it seems to be effectively appreciated only from an elitist perspective on the order of Lanny Budd's. To alternately see the world from Lanny's "inside" position and then from the position, say, of a member of the European lower classes was not Sinclair's choice. In the Lanny Budd novels, the focus that Sinclair used so effectively in *The Jungle* is reversed. Lanny is the Jurgis Rudkus of the upper class, and his adventures, like Jurgis's, are significant for what they reveal about the class he represents.

CHAPTER 11

End of a Career

THE last phase of Sinclair's writing career comprised the years from 1950 to 1962. In 1950 Sinclair was seventy-two years old and certainly had reason to consider himself at least semi-retired, especially after the three million word effort of the first ten volumes of the Lanny Budd story. Yet Sinclair's typewriter showed few signs of stopping. It slowed down somewhat from the energetic pace of the forties, and turned out books that were generally less strident and more nostalgic. In addition to *The Return of Lanny Budd* in 1953, which followed the tenth volume of the series by four years, Sinclair wrote and published six other significant books after 1950[1]—three novels, a biography of Jesus, a polemical collection of essays about his alcoholic friends, and an expanded version of his autobiography—in addition to lesser pamphlets, articles, plays, and letters.

During these later years of his career and even up to his death in 1968, Sinclair's life was publicly tranquil. No longer did he maintain much of a quarrel with the shape of American politics. In fact, in the early fifties Sinclair spoke out against the more extreme critics of McCarthyism, pointing out that McCarthy was hardly as threatening as was Communism.[2] Later he failed to agitate support for the Civil Rights movement in any of his publications; and towards the end of his life he found himself in support of American policy in Vietnam, again because of his fear of Communist domination.[3] In addition to his general approval of the American scene, Sinclair enjoyed the role of a historical figure. Not recognized as a literary great, he was nevertheless held in respect, increasingly becoming the subject of Ph.D. dissertations, giving interviews concerning his work in the past, honored by the labor movement and by many liberals, and invited by President Johnson to be present at the signing of the Meat Inspection Bill in 1967.

Privately during these years Sinclair's life contained a measure of sorrow. His wife Mary Craig, who since 1913 had served often as his editor, business manager, and sometimes collaborator, was bedridden from 1954 to 1961 with a painful and eventually fatal heart disease. For seven years Sinclair himself willingly served twenty-four hour duty as "nurse, cook, housemaid, chauffeur, and guardian angel."[4]

Perhaps as a result of both the non-contentious nature of his public life and the sadness of his wife's illness and death, Sinclair's later writings offer not only a mellowing of the old radical fervor but also a tinge of religious acceptance. Sinclair's basic religiosity had been present in his work ever since "Unity and Infinity in Art" in 1899, but had usually been a combination of seeking to explain existence through the holistic concept of economic determinism and accepting the personal role of inspired evangelist; Christianity, in particular, for Sinclair, had been a "fighting faith" in favor of social justice, and had implied the distinct possibility of achieving the kingdom of God on earth in the form of the Cooperative Commonwealth or of democratic Socialism. After 1950, tones of acceptance and even pessimism were audible but not loud in his expressions.

I *From Pamela to Didymus*

Sinclair's writings in the fifties and sixties, in general, are chiefly important for what they reveal about his life, his sensibility, or his times. These ends are especially apparent of *The Cup of Fury* (1956), his book on alcoholism, and even more so of *The Autobiography of Upton Sinclair* (1962). *A Personal Jesus* (1952) also seems to be an exposition of Sinclair's attitudes more than an exploration of the nature and meaning of Jesus. He published three novels—*Another Pamela* (1950), *It Happened to Didymus* (1958, but published in England in 1954 as *What Didymus Did*), and *Affectionately, Eve* (1961)—which are valuable both biographically and, in varying degrees, intrinsically.

In *Another Pamela* Sinclair chose to revive the basic narrative technique he had used forty-seven years earlier in *The Journal of Arthur Stirling* and to apply it to a different social context with an entirely different kind of protagonist. In 1903 he had told the story of his suicidal young poet in a fictional journal; in 1950, in his story of a pietistical young country girl, he relied on fictional letters written by his heroine to her sister and mother. In a most obvious way, Sinclair attempted to recast Samuel Richardson's *Pamela* (1740) into a modern situation, complete with an awareness of social classes in

America and a belief in the ability of spirit to bridge the cultural gaps created by wealth.

The novel is, for Sinclair, witty, pleasant, and mostly reflective rather than ideological. As generally admiring reviewers noted, Sinclair was "far too clever and serious to write a mere imitation"[5] of Richardson's eighteenth century work. His Pamela Andrews is at first a teenage goat herder, the daughter of a nearly destitute rural California family whose father has died; she happens also to be a strict Seventh-Day Adventist. Pamela, sixteen when the novel begins, in 1919, is hired as a parlor maid by a wealthy Mrs. Harries, a socially minded philanthropist who dispenses money to radical causes and opens her mansion on Sunday afternoons to lectures by persons as various as I.W.W. leaders and religious poets. Mrs. Harries's existence, however, is far from pleasant; she must abide a reactionary and vocal husband as well as an adopted (and pampered) nephew who is alienated, alcoholic, and promiscuous. As the story develops, the good-hearted but unhappy nephew, Charles, finds Pamela sexually attractive and attempts continually to seduce her. Cleverly, Sinclair has Pamela recognize Charles's need for help; and rather than avoid him completely, she allows his advances up to a point in order to present her ideas of virtue and religion to him. Obviously attracted to Charles, Pamela experiences a conflict of flesh and spirit, as she reveals in long letters to her sister:

I like his hand, and a lovely feeling steals over me when he takes it in mine. But also I am frightened by my feelings, and I think, what is he going to do now, and can this be right? I have never in my life been so mixed up about anything. I say, this is temptation; this car is temptation, and this lovely ride; the devil is after me. But if I can save this young man from getting drunk again, will not that be a victory over Satan? I try to put myself in Satan's place and guess which he would prefer, to have me being kissed or to have Master Charles drunk. I fear I am not very good at taking Satan's place, for I never wanted to hurt anybody in my life, and it is hard for me to imagine such an attitude as malice.[6]

Pamela's conflict is resolved when she is finally able to convince Charles of the existence of God—or at least of some kind of reigning purpose in the universe—and wean him of the bottle. She does not, however, immediately jump at the chance of marriage into a wealthy family when Charles finally proposes to her; intelligently aware that Charles might later convince himself that she had demanded marriage in order to gain access to his money, she also requires that she be allowed to keep her position within the Harries's household, where she has become Mrs. Harries's secretary.

The Viking Press advertised *Another Pamela* as "a departure from anything that even this versatile author had ever offered us before," a statement only half correct. The novel is essentially a comedy of manners, and it focuses largely on the difference between Pamela's kind of proletarian life and the affluent ways of the Harries family. Sinclair had often attempted this kind of contrast—in fact, almost all of his novels before the Lanny Budd series include a similar focus. But his presentation of the wealthy had never been as convincing as in *Another Pamela*. Pamela approves of Mrs. Harries's radical causes, but she also realizes the unhappiness and personal conflicts in the family: "Underneath all the disharmony in this family is the money, which is a terrible power"(209). The corrupting power of wealth is the oldest Sinclair theme. Seldom, however, had he been able to show the coexistence of such corruption with basic good intentions and social consciences.

The resolution in the novel is gently forced, with Charles having to make the greater compromise in closing the cultural gap between him and Pamela. Pamela begins to apply her fundamentalistic religious ideas in a broader context, seeing that Christianity should lead to here and now reform, saying to Charles that "Jesus taught us that the Kingdom of God is within you." Eventually, she even breaks the rules of her faith by attending movies. Charles, in addition to having to recognize a lower-class girl as more than a sexual object, must convert himself from a rather sophisticated and intelligent atheism to a willingness to try Pamela's faith.

The strengths of *Another Pamela* lie in Sinclair's objective awareness of cultural differences stemming from socio-economic origins, and in his epistolary form. There are suggestions of *The Adventures of Huckleberry Finn* in the author's willingness to eliminate his own voice and speak through a persona who is at first awkward in both manners and literary style. By adopting this persona, Sinclair eliminated the necessity of creating the often bothersome omniscience of other novels. Pamela's letters to her sister and her mother are convincing and intriguing; and her story is an obvious contrast to the plutocratic perspectives of Lanny Budd. It is unfortunate that Sinclair did not attempt this technique in some of his earlier novels involving strong male protagonists of proletarian origin.

In 1961 Sinclair returned to his epistolary format in *Affectionately,*

Eve, another novel of letters written by a young woman. Eve Forrester, however, is the daughter of an established Southern family rather than the lower class. Her letters concern her mission in New York City, where she had come to commission a sculpture to commemorate the Confederate Woman. Like Pamela Andrews, Eve is introduced to advanced ideas, especially in the form of a sculptor who wishes to use her as the model for the statue—an idea which Eve at first finds repelling because she thinks the folks at home will interpret it as an act of egotism on her part. Eventually she falls in love in the North to an unhappily married research scientist rather than to an alienated millionaire and, after her lover manages a divorce, marries him.[7]

Affectionately, Eve is a light and pleasant novel which again deals with the clash of cultural assumptions. Eve's most difficult problem is presenting herself and her adventures to her family. The novel raises far less serious questions than does *Another Pamela.* Eve's story is a veiled retelling of the early life of Sinclair's wife Mary Craig, a self-described "Southern Belle" (the title of her autobiography) who went to finishing school in New York City and became the friend of radicals before World War I.[8] One such radical—and an already married one—was Sinclair. Mary Craig Sinclair died in the same year that *Affectionately, Eve* was published, and Sinclair may have created his novel as a kind of memorial to both Mary Craig's personality and to the tensions within it. As such, and because his own career had been shaped by a combination of Southern roots and advanced ideas, it was a fitting expression.

In *It Happened to Didymus,* published first in 1954 after the enormously successful Lanny Budd books, Sinclair offers unusual self-criticism of his efforts as a reformer. In this novel, produced near the end of his career as a writer of fiction (only *Affectionately, Eve* came afterward), the possibility of social reform, particularly through revolutionary change, is viewed through a lens of almost overt pessimism. (To some extent this kind of skepticism about social reform may be related to Sinclair's serious disenchantment with Soviet Communism in the late forties and early fifties rather than with any doubts about his own career as a reformer.) As with many other Sinclair books, *It Happened to Didymus* also involves religion, and is obviously infused with Sinclair's own strong religious bent; but in this case the religiosity of the novel is one of skeptical acceptance of human nature rather than of eager crusading for social justice.

The story, which as a narrative never approaches the interest of

Another Pamela, is a fantasy involving a young man named Thomas (*Didymus* in Greek) who is visited by an angel and thereafter has the power to order miracles at his convenience. A reformer of extreme hopes, Didymus wishes to rid America of vice and drunkenness; he says to others, "I am sent to proclaim a new order to the world, a new birth of the spirit."[9] Such words seem ironically like echoes from the pages of *Springtime and Harvest, Prince Hagen,* or *The Journal of Arthur Stirling.* The point of Sinclair's 1954 story, however, concerns the rather limited effectiveness of the spiritual sources that allow Didymus to perform miracles. Didymus tries to reform human nature in Los Angeles, but in the end he fails, and his supernatural powers desert him. At the end of the novel Sinclair's narrator and voice, a high school teacher who tends to admire Didymus' basic intentions, says conservatively that "We have brought ourselves to realize that human organisms have taken a long time to evolve, perhaps a million years, while civilizations have had only a few thousand. There is no thinking they can be forced. The people of Los Angeles will have to go on groping and blundering and learn by suffering, since nature or God has provided no other way" (150–51).

This passage hardly sounds like the muckraker, Socialist, publicist, or left-wing politician that Sinclair had so often been since 1900. *Didymus* is therefore a difficult expression to understand within the context of Sinclair's career. Perhaps it is best to consider the novel as less than a final or even penultimate analysis, and to define it as simply a moment of doubt when, after watching the development of atomic weapons and the apparently grave Cold War conflict between capitalist America and Communist Russia, Sinclair found time to consider whether reformers of his own energetic type were sometimes a bit too hopeful. Eight years after *Didymus,* in his 1962 autobiography, he reasserted his earlier positive faith, saying "I don't know whether anyone will care to examine my heart, but if they do they will find two words there—'Social Justice.' For this is what I have believed in and fought for during sixty-three of my eighty-four years."[10]

CHAPTER 12

Conclusion

WHEN Sinclair died in November of 1968 he was ninety years old. He had been born in the Gilded Age, and he had grown up in the turbulent urban America of the 1880's and 1890's. Out of his Southern roots and traditional influences he had become a literary rebel and political spokesman during the Progressive Era of American history. In *The Jungle* he had stirred the conscience of the world, influenced the course of national legislation, and produced a permanent impact on American life. During the twenties he had remained a domestic social critic without giving up his Socialist political expectations. During the Great Depression he had been looked to for answers and had responded with his EPIC movement and more than a dozen books. For millions of readers during and following World War II he had served as the interpreter of twentieth century history. In the fifties and sixties, having in some ways lived quite beyond his time, he had retained his garrulous but always clear voice.

Never a great writer in the terms of style and structure, never a symbolist or a modernist, interested in the external affairs of society and politics rather than in the internal affairs of human consciousness, journalistic and populistic rather than poetic and eloquent, Sinclair remains a problem for literary historians and critics. The problem is greatest for those critics who refuse either to dismiss Sinclair as an important writer—that is, for those who recognize the extent of his influence and respect the energy and idealism behind his rhetoric— or to dismiss his literary deficiencies.

This study has attempted to discuss Sinclair's works, particularly his most important novels, not only as individual literary efforts but also as the phenomena and evidence of his unique career. The picture of Sinclair that emerges is that of a nineteenth century moral idealist somewhat ill at ease in the twentieth century but almost totally

155

committed to the exploration and, where possible, reform of the world around him. Consequently, Sinclair's attention, in novel after novel, to the problems of community—particularly the relationship of the politically radical individual to the community or society of which he necessarily forms a part—as well as to the meanings of history appear to be points of particular significance and relevance within his career.

More specific, more sympathetic, or more critical interpretations are possible. Sinclair can be seen, as Robert Cantwell saw him in the thirties, as a modern iconoclast who wrote against the "genteel tradition" in American letters and who thereby widened the scope and effectiveness of twentieth century fiction.[1] He can also been seen as an exaggerated paradigm of the Progressive Era of American history, a figure who believed aggressively that the cure for the failings of civilization lay in the application of even more civilization in the form of a technologically oriented Socialism.[2] Or it may be appropriate to understand Sinclair as the kind of wide ranging, inherently pragmatic, and indigenously American radical that Justin Kaplan has seen in Lincoln Steffens;[3] or as a displaced Southern aristocrat seeking his identity and function in an industrial society; or as a misguided political theorist and propagandist whose ideas were based mostly on an acceptance of Manichean, conspiratorial forces in politics and history;[4] or simply as a crusader for social justice, a man of heart rather than mind. All of these ways of perceiving Sinclair are functional, and each reveals another facet of an intriguing and sometimes exasperating American man of letters.

No approach to Sinclair, no consideration of his works, should neglect his most basic contribution to the world of literature: a strongly expressed sensitivity to inequities in the political and social life of modern capitalistic society. Although this sensitivity is particularly strong in some works and only barely apparent in others, it is still Sinclair's most salient feature. Other writers in the course of Western civilization have of course been acutely aware of injustice, and many have written compassionately in the cause of civil and economic rights. But no writer ever made these matters so exclusively his or her *raison d'être* as Sinclair did. Even within a larger realization of his literary weaknesses and intellectual ambivalences, and taking into account even his blindness to racial oppression, Sinclair's commitment to social justice commands respect.

This commitment has had its influence on American culture. Early in his career, especially between the publication of *The Jungle* in

1906 and the shock of World War I, Sinclair was an important and respected member of a school of American writers—including Frank Norris (though deceased by 1906), Jack London, and Theodore Dreiser—who helped shape the social criticism of later and quite different writers. *"The Jungle* and *The Octopus* were on our shelves before John Steinbeck ate the grapes of wrath," F. Scott Fitzgerald once said of his own generation of writers.[5]

Fitzgerald's words suggest a shaping power in Sinclair's writings that has continued beyond the twenties and thirties. Often disdained by more modernistic intellectuals, and generally ignored by literary scholarship in the United States, Sinclair's works have nevertheless survived to be read and to produce often striking effects. In his 1975 biography of Sinclair, Leon Harris lists statements by contemporary American figures who were influenced, in one way or another, by Sinclair. These include Robert McNamara, Allen Ginsberg, Daniel Patrick Moynihan, Walter Cronkite, and Norman Mailer.[6] The social and political effects of Sinclair's books, from the Pure Food and Drug Act of 1906 to the consumer movement of the 1970's, is yet to be fully measured.

For many years, up to World War II in particular, Sinclair was also one of the most widely read American writers abroad. He and Jack London have been translated into literally dozens of languages. In Sinclair's case, part of this overseas interest was possibly due to the ease of translating his prose. But another—and more important part—is due to the dominance of fact and the delineation of America in his books. Consequently, in European letters Sinclair has exerted a noticeable influence. George Bernard Shaw was a close literary friend of Sinclair's. Bertolt Brecht not only read Sinclair but was also in touch with the American muckraker through a mutual friend.[7] Herbert Marcuse, intellectual leader in the so-called New Left movement of the late sixties and early seventies, remembers having read "almost all of Upton Sinclair's books, quite a few of them prior to my coming to the United States in 1934. I can say that they gave me a new and very powerful picture of this country."[8]

Today, with the exception of *The Jungle,* Sinclair's literary reputation is small, his influence on new writers practically nothing. His main significance is historical, and his historical significance is enhanced not only because of his involvement with American political life, but also because he wrote so often about his involvement. He is eminently accessible in his books, his public and private experiences more a matter of printed record than those of most historical figures. But the main body of teachers and scholars of American literature treat him with respectful neglect.

This is perhaps as it should be. *The Jungle* rightfully continues to be a part of the reading experience of Americans. Most of Sinclair's other works will either be read by readers who are intrigued by *The Jungle* or they will not. Those who read much of Sinclair will undoubtedly be bothered at times by his unsophisticated style and the occasional shallowness and confusion of his thought. Some will regard his literary efforts as overly utilitarian, servants of causes now gone rather than explorations of universal problems; others will see that Sinclair failed to understand that great literature does not simplify, but instead reveals life as complex and difficult to fathom.

But those who read on may also be impressed by Sinclair's effort to make literature functional. In one of his earliest essays, "Our Bourgeois Literature," he voiced disapproval of writing which seemed to honor the realm of spirit or taste or aesthetics as separate from the realm of ordinary reality. In his politics he was also disturbed by the tendency of Americans to honor the words, documents, and symbols of democracy without seeming to be overly concerned about widespread injustice. His political attitudes were ideals in the service of reality. His writings, for the most part, were art in the service of human needs. These needs, the objects of his propaganda, included the basic eighteenth century concept of inalienable rights in the individual. They also included economic rights, a concern which recent writers of a more affluent society have tended to neglect.

Notes and References

Preface

1. Alfred Kazin, *On Native Grounds* (New York, 1956), p. 89.
2. Louis Filler, *The Muckrakers: Crusaders for American Liberalism* (Chicago, 1968), p. 121.
3. Howard Mumford Jones, *The Age of Energy: Varieties of American Experience, 1865–1914* (New York, 1971), p. 8.
4. Kazin, pp. 91–92.

Chapter One

1. Especially *The Autobiography of Upton Sinclair* (New York, 1962), but also an autobiographical novel, *Love's Pilgrimage* (New York, 1911).
2. *Love's Pilgrimage*, p. 4.
3. *Autobiography*, pp. 7–9.
4. *Ibid.*, p. 8.
5. Sinclair's relationship (or lack of relationship) with his father may have been a contributing factor to his later anti-capitalist attitudes. As an adult Sinclair obviously disapproved of the kind of lifestyle his father had earlier exhibited. In *Childhood and Society* (New York, 1963), p. 258, Erik Erikson mentions the way in which typical "Oedipal" feelings—a mingling of jealousy and respect—actually motivate sons to *follow* the ways of their fathers and thus continue the economic ethos of their culture. This does not seem to have happened in Sinclair's case.
6. Sinclair, *The Cup of Fury* (New York, 1956), p. 24. This book, a collection of essays on famous alcoholics Sinclair knew, includes some information about his early years and his relationship with his father.
7. *Autobiography*, p. 29.
8. David Riesman, *The Lonely Crowd*, abridged ed. (New Haven, 1961), p. 89.
9. *Autobiography*, p. 16; *Love's Pilgrimage*, p. 8.
10. *Autobiography*, p. 17.

11. Sinclair, *The Goose-Step* (Pasadena, 1923), pp. 4–9. This book, an examination of American higher education, also recounts much of Sinclair's own educational experience.

12. *Autobiography*, p. 35. Many of Sinclair's jokes exist in a scrapbook kept by his mother and now part of the Sinclair Archives in the Lilly Library of Indiana University.

13. This story is summarized in Ronald Gottesman, "Upton Sinclair: An Annotated Bibliographical Catalogue, 1894–1932," diss. Indiana 1964.

14. *Autobiography*, p. 31.

15. *Love's Pilgrimage*, pp. 24–25.

16. *Ibid.*, pp. 64–65.

17. *Ibid.*, pp. 10–11.

18. William James and Jane Addams are two well-known examples.

19. *Cup of Fury*, p. 26.

20. This is a large part of his message in *The Profits of Religion* (Pasadena, 1918).

21. *Autobiography*, pp. 53–54.

22. *Cup of Fury*, p. 15.

23. Sinclair, "MacDowell," *American Mercury* (January 1926), pp. 50, 52, 54.

24. George Edward Woodberry, *Literary Essays* (New York, 1920), p. 118.

25. *Autobiography*, pp. 49–52.

26. Lt. Frederick Garrison (pseud.), "The Populist Trust Hunters; or How Sleepy Was Converted," *Half-Holiday* (16 July 1898), pp. 1–5. (*Half-Holiday* was one of several juvenile magazines published by Street and Smith.)

27. Sinclair, "Unity and Infinity in Art," *The Metaphysical Magazine* (January 1899), p. 8.

28. *Ibid.*, pp. 16–17.

29. *Love's Pilgrimage*, p. 44. Also see *Autobiography*, pp. 70–71. In his recent biography of Sinclair, Leon Harris sheds new light on Sinclair's dissatisfaction around 1900. In a 1931 letter to his son, quoted by Harris, Sinclair said of his mother, "She was the best of mothers up to about the age (my age) of 16. Then I grew beyond her, & she wouldn't follow, or couldn't. If she'd let me alone, it could have been all right; but she still thought I was a child & stubbornly fought to direct my life & *mind* . . . my mother never had a gleam of interest in any of my ideals—never anything but holding me to & for herself." Leon Harris, *Upton Sinclair: American Rebel* (New York, 1975), p. 99.

Chapter Two

1. *Autobiography*, p. 71.

2. *Love's Pilgrimage*, pp. 13–16.

3. *Ibid.*, pp. 13–65. The odd details of this marriage—including Meta's apparent hopes that Sinclair could bring out her own artistic proclivities—are documented extensively in Harris's biography; they are also largely available in Sinclair's autobiography and in *Love's Pilgrimage*. In the novel they seem more truthful.

4. *Autobiography*, p. 71.

5. Sinclair, *King Midas* (New York, 1901), p. 225. *King Midas* is a retitled and reissued version of *Springtime and Harvest*. *Springtime and Harvest* was published privately early in 1901 and for this reason is a rather rare text.

6. *Love's Pilgrimage*, pp. 202–204. Again, Harris's biography reveals extensively the incredible emotional problems created by Sinclair's egotistical literary hopes and Meta's equally egotistical striving for her own needs; in places Harris also adds information from sources besides Sinclair's published works, which are, however, remarkably candid about his first marriage.

7. Sinclair, *Springtime and Harvest: A Romance* (New York, 1901), introduction (n.p.).

8. *Love's Pilgrimage*, pp. 157–58.

9. Sinclair, *Prince Hagen: A Phantasy* (Boston, 1903), pp. 13–14.

10. *Love's Pilgrimage*, pp. 259–63.

11. Sinclair, *The Overman* (New York, 1907), in various places.

12. *Love's Pilgrimage*, p. 13.

13. *Autobiography*, pp. 86–87.

14. Sinclair, *The Journal of Arthur Stirling* (New York, 1903).

15. "The Confessions of a Young Author," *Independent*, 54 (20 Nov. 1902), 2748–52.

16. *Autobiography*, p. 100.

17. *Ibid.*, p. 101.

18. Charles H. Hopkins, *The Rise of the Social Gospel in American Protestantism, 1865–1915* (New Haven, 1940), pp. 184–200.

19. *Love's Pilgrimage*, p. 417.

20. Sinclair, *A Captain of Industry* (Girard, Kansas, 1906).

21. Arthur B. Maurice, *Bookman*, March 1903, pp. 84–85.

22. Sinclair, "My Cause," *Independent*, 55 (14 May 1903), 1121–26.

23. Sinclair, *Manassas* (New York, 1904).

24. This search is explained in Harold S. Wilson, *McClure's Magazine and the Muckrakers* (Princeton, 1970).

25. Sinclair, "Every Man His Own Reviewer," *Independent*, 57 (17 Nov. 1904), 1150.

Chapter Three

1. Sinclair, "You Have Lost the Strike! And Now What Are You Going to Do About It?" *Appeal to Reason* (17 Sept. 1904), p. 1; "The Spirit That Wins," *Appeal* (24 Sept. 1904), p. 3; and "Farmers of America, Unite!" *Appeal* (15 Oct. 1904), pp. 2–3.

2. Sinclair, "The Socialist Party: Its Aims in the Present Campaign," *Collier's* (29 Oct. 1904), pp. 10, 12.

3. Sinclair, "Our Bourgeois Literature: The Reason and the Remedy," *Collier's* (8 Oct. 1904), pp. 22–25.

4. As quoted in Harris, *Upton Sinclair*, p. 78.

5. Sinclair, *Appeal to Reason* (11 Feb. 1905), p. 1.

6. Harris, pp. 78–79.

7. *Autobiography*, p. 112.

8. Sinclair, "What Life Means to Me," *Cosmopolitan*, 41 (Oct. 1906), 594.

9. Sinclair, *The Jungle* (New York, 1960), p. 20. Following parenthetical references are from this New American Library paperback which is more accessible than the first edition of the novel.

10. Details of publishing are carefully explained in Ronald Gottesman, "Upton Sinclair: An Annotated Bibliographical Catalogue," diss. Indiana, 1964.

11. The ending of *The Jungle* has been perceptively analyzed in Michael B. Folsom, "Literary Radicalism and Genteel Tradition: A Study of the Principal Literary Works of the American Socialist Movement Before 1912," diss. California (Berkeley) 1972.

12. Harris, p. 75.

13. *Autobiography*, p. 112.

14. John Braeman, "The Square Deal in Action: A Case Study in the Growth of the 'National Police Power,' " in Braeman, *et al, Change and Continuity in Twentieth-Century America* (Columbus, 1964), p. 45.

15. Waverly Root and Richard de Rochemont, *Eating in America: A History* (New York, 1976), pp. 210–11.

16. Sinclair, "What Life Means to Me," p. 594.

17. *Ibid.*

18. Harvey Swados, "The World of Upton Sinclair," *Atlantic Monthly* (Dec. 1961), pp. 96–102.

19. Larzer Ziff, *The American 1890s: Life and Times of a Lost Generation* (New York, 1966), p. 348.

20. Mike Gold, *Jews Without Money* (New York, 1965), p. 154. (Gold's novel was first published in 1930.)

21. For this point I am much indebted to Michael Folsom's analysis in "Literary Radicalism and Genteel Tradition."

Chapter Four

1. Harris, *Upton Sinclair*, p. 84. Harris also provides an interesting general discussion of *The Jungle*'s reception.

2. Sinclair, *Money Writes!* (Pasadena, 1927), p. 127.

3. Details of Sinclair's interest in meat packing legislation in 1906 can be

found in John Braeman, "The Square Deal in Action: A Case Study in the Growth of the 'National Police Power,' " in Braeman, *et al., Change and Continuity in Twentieth-Century America* (Columbus, 1964), pp. 35–80.

4. Especially "Stockyards Secrets," *Collier's* (24 March 1906); "The Socialist Party," *World's Work* (April 1906); "Is the *Jungle* True?" *Independent*, 55 (17 May 1906); "The Condemned Meat Industry," *Everybody's Magazine* (May 1906); and "What Life Means to Me," *Cosmopolitan* (Oct. 1906).

5. Sinclair, *The Brass Check* (Pasadena, 1920), pp. 55–57.

6. Sinclair, *The Industrial Republic* (New York, 1907).

7. *The Brass Check*, p. 67.

8. *Autobiography*, p. 138. Sinclair's wife, then suffering from appendicitis and from recurring menstrual difficulties, spent time here.

9. Sinclair, *The Metropolis* (New York, 1908), p. 376.

10. *Autobiography*, p. 139.

11. Sinclair, *The Moneychangers* (New York, 1908), p. 316.

12. "Spookology" is used by Albert Mordell in *Haldeman-Julius and Upton Sinclair: The Amazing Record of a Long Collaboration* (Girard, 1950). Some of Sinclair's works which deal with the bizarre, the mystical, or the occult are "Unity and Infinity in Art" (1899), *The Fasting Cure* (1911), *The Book of Life* (1922), and *Mental Radio* (1930).

13. Sinclair's efforts as a playwright have been examined in C. C. Heimerdinger, "Propagandist in the Theatre: The Career of Upton Sinclair as a Dramatist," diss. Indiana 1968.

14. In *Plays of Protest* (New York, 1912).

15. *Ibid.*

16. *Autobiography*, p. 157.

17. Sinclair, *Samuel the Seeker* (New York, 1910), p. 1.

18. *Autobiography*, pp. 75, 164.

19. *Love's Pilgrimage*, p. 470. References to this novel are indicated parenthetically.

20. Critical response to the novel was mixed. Conservative readers tended to think that it was too sensational. For instance, the psychologist G. Stanley Hall, whom Sinclair asked to read the book, said in a letter that he would not allow a young friend of either sex to read it. Others, like Brand Whitlock and Floyd Dell, felt that it was a courageous book. Letters from these persons to Sinclair are in the Sinclair Archives.

21. Sinclair, *Damaged Goods* (Philadelphia, 1913). Sinclair revised Brieux's plot somewhat by having the protagonist feel sorry for being unfaithful as well as having contracted and spread venereal disease.

22. Sinclair, *Sylvia* (Philadelphia, 1913), p. 175.

23. Sinclair, *Sylvia's Marriage* (Philadelphia, 1914), p. 88.

24. Sinclair, *The Millennium* (Girard, 1924). Reprinted by Sinclair himself in 1929. Originally published in the *Appeal to Reason* (18 April to 1 August 1914).

Chapter Five

1. Sinclair, "A Christmas Letter," *New York Call*, 3 Jan. 1914.
2. Vincent Astor to Sinclair, 10 Jan. 1914, Sinclair Archives.
3. Sinclair to Vincent Astor, 19 Jan. 1914, Sinclair Archives.
4. *Autobiography*, pp. 198–201.
5. Sinclair to John D. Rockefeller, Jr., 26 May 1914, Sinclair Archives.
6. Sinclair, *The Cry for Justice* (Philadelphia, 1915).
7. James Burkhart Gilbert, *Writers and Partisans* (New York, 1968), p. 10.
8. Printed letter of 25 May 1915, Sinclair Archives. It should be pointed out that Sinclair later revised his judgment of Rockefeller and in his autobiography even praises the family for its acceptance of social responsibility (p. 202).
9. George P. Brett to Sinclair, 31 Dec. 1915, Sinclair Archives.
10. Brett to Sinclair, 9 May 1916, Sinclair Archives.
11. Mary Craig Sinclair, *Southern Belle* (New York, 1957), pp. 111–12.
12. *Autobiography*, p. 212.
13. Sinclair, *King Coal* (New York, 1917), pp. 55–57.
14. This is Floyd Dell's opinion in *Upton Sinclair: A Study in Social Protest* (New York, 1927).

Chapter Six

1. Henry F. May, *An End to Innocence: A Study of the First Years of Our Time, 1912–1917* (Chicago, 1964), p. 393.
2. Walter B. Rideout, *The Radical Novel in the United States* (New York, 1956), p. 38.
3. Sinclair had indicated his desire to publish his own books as early as May 1903 in his *Independent* article entitled "My Cause." His stated purpose was to make available the kind of books that regular publishers often felt would not sell. Undoubtedly, much of his anxiety over trade publishers grew out of his memory of demands made on him when he was a hack writer for juvenile publications; also, the failure of several of his books to be accepted readily by regular publishers made him wary of the publishing industry. It should be remembered that his first serious novel was published privately. In any event, from 1918, when he published *The Profits of Religion*, until 1949, Sinclair published most of his own books. Usually he made arrangements with a publishing house to issue the book also, at the same time, under its imprint. Many books, though, especially his pamphlets, were published only by Sinclair himself in Pasadena. By doing this Sinclair was able not only to get his works before his public, but also to do so in very inexpensive editions, many of which were paperbound.
4. Sinclair, "War: A Manifesto Against It," *Wilshire's Magazine* (Sept. 1910), p. 7.

5. Sinclair received persuasive letters from Van Eeden on 30 August; 9 Sept.; 14 Sept.; and 12 Oct. 1914. Herron wrote on 25 Oct., and Kropotkin on 23 Dec. These letters are in the Sinclair Archives.

6. Sinclair, "Letter of Resignation," Chicago *Sunday Tribune* (22 July 1917), Part 8, p. 5.

7. Stanley K. Schultz's introduction to a reprinted edition of *Upton Sinclair's* (Westport, Conn., 1970) provides an excellent analysis of the journal as well as critical insight into the ambivalent nature of Sinclair's radicalism within its pages.

8. Sinclair, "A Telegram for Russia," *Upton Sinclair's* (Aug. 1918), p. 5.

9. Sinclair, "The Problem of Russia," *Upton Sinclair's* (Oct. 1918), p. 5.

10. Sinclair, "What About Bolshevism?" *Upton Sinclair's* (Jan. 1919), p. 4.

11. Sinclair, *Jimmie Higgins* (Lexington, 1970), p. 227. This text, reprinted from the original 1919 plates, has an excellent introduction by David A. Shannon and may be more available than the original edition.

12. Sinclair, *100%: The Story of a Patriot* (Pasadena, 1920), dust jacket.

13. Rideout, *The Radical Novel in the United States*, p. 87.

14. Sinclair, *They Call Me Carpenter* (Pasadena, 1922).

15. Sinclair, *The Book of Life* (Pasadena, 1922), pp. 218–219.

16. Floyd Dell, *Upton Sinclair* (New York, 1927), p. 167.

17. F. Scott Fitzgerald, *The Crack-Up*, ed. Edmund Wilson (New York, 1945), p. 257.

18. Sinclair, *Mammonart* (Pasadena, 1925), p. 275.

19. Lewis A. Fretz, "Upton Sinclair: The Don Quixote of American Reform," diss. Stanford 1970, p. 88.

Chapter Seven

1. Dell, *Upton Sinclair*, p. 178.

2. *Independent*, 118 (9 April 1927), 393.

3. William McFee, "Americana," *New Republic*, 51 (15 June 1927), 104.

4. Sinclair, *Oil!* (New York, 1927), pp. 526–27.

5. Johan Smertenko, "Upton Sinclair at His Best," *Nation*, 124 (8 June 1927), 644.

6. Michael Millgate, *American Social Fiction* (New York, 1964), pp. 68–69.

Chapter Eight

1. Fredrick J. Hoffman, *The Twenties: American Writing in the Postwar Decade*, rev. ed. (New York, 1962), p. 400.

2. This is the verdict of G. Louis Joughin in Joughin and Edmund M. Morgan, *The Legacy of Sacco and Vanzetti* (New York, 1948), pp. 445–53.

3. In my account of the case I have relied on the following sources:

Hoffman's brief analysis, pp. 400–408; Joughin and Morgan, pp. 3–197; Daniel Aaron's *Writers on the Left* (New York, 1965), pp. 185–90; "The Story of the Case" in *The Letters of Sacco and Vanzetti*, ed. Marian D. Frankfurter and Gardner Jackson (New York, 1928), pp. 329–60; and Felix Frankfurter, *The Case of Sacco and Vanzetti: A Critical Analysis for Lawyers and Laymen* (Boston, 1927).

4. Frankfurter, *The Case of Sacco and Vanzetti*, p. 97.

5. Hoffman, *The Twenties*, p. 403.

6. I have quoted this passage from Sinclair, *Boston* (Pasadena, 1928), p. 615, where Sinclair identifies it as a reporter's transcript of an interview with Vanzetti and mentions that it has often been mistakenly accepted (as Hoffman accepts it) as part of Vanzetti's speech at his sentencing. This is typical of Sinclair's devotion to accurate fact in the novel.

7. Hoffman, *The Twenties*, p. 404.

8. Malcolm Cowley, "For St. Bartholomew's Day," *Nation*, 127 (22 Aug. 1928), 175.

9. Joughin and Morgan, *The Legacy of Sacco and Vanzetti*, p. 439.

10. Daniel, *Writers on the Left*, p. 187.

11. Sinclair, "Vanzetti—A Tribute and an Appeal," *Appeal to Reason* (17 June 1922), p. 1; and "Now As in the Days of Henry D. Thoreau, Massachusetts Has Its Greatest Soul in Jail," *New York American* (16 Sept. 1923), p. 3.

12. Sinclair, *Autobiography*, p. 240.

13. Sinclair, *Boston*, p. v.

14. Alice Stone Blackwell and Glendower Evans.

15. This would be the Willett case, which was described in Felix Frankfurter and James M. Lundis, "Bankers and the Conspiracy Laws," *New Republic*, 41 (21 Jan. 1925), 218–20.

16. Leon Harris points out that, according to private correspondence, Sinclair had serious doubts about Sacco's innocence and may even have eventually doubted Vanzetti's. *Upton Sinclair: American Rebel*, p. 246. However, there is no evidence that he ever regarded the legal procedures involved as anything but a travesty of justice.

Chapter Nine

1. Sinclair's inconsistent political notions are more than adequately described in Fretz's dissertation, "Upton Sinclair: The Don Quixote of American Reform."

2. *Our Lady* (Pasadena, 1938).

3. Sinclair and Eugene Lyons, *Terror in Russia?* (New York, 1938).

4. Gottesman mentions this in his dissertation, "Upton Sinclair: An Annotated Bibliographical Catalogue, 1894–1932," diss. Indiana 1964.

5. C. Hartley Grattan, "Autobiography of an Idealist," *Nation*, 134 (13 April 1932), 433.

6. Sinclair, *Money Writes!* (Pasadena, 1927), p. 222.

7. Gilbert, *Writers and Partisans*, p. 77.

8. Sinclair, "How Accurate Was the *Digest* Poll?" *New Republic*, 63 (13 Aug. 1930), 373–74.

9. H. L. Mencken, "A Moral Tale," *Nation*, 133 (23 Sept. 1931), p. 310.

10. Mary Craig Sinclair, "A Letter from Mary Craig Sinclair to Eve Fox," p. 7, published as an insert in Sinclair, *Upton Sinclair Presents William Fox* (Los Angeles, 1933).

11. Sinclair, *The Way Out: What Lies Ahead for America* (Pasadena, 1933), p. xii.

12. *Ibid.*, pp. 107–8.

13. Arthur M. Schlesinger, Jr., *The Politics of Upheaval*, vol. 3 of *The Age of Roosevelt* (Boston, 1960), pp. 109–24.

14. Sinclair, *Co-Op: A Novel of Living Together* (Pasadena, 1936).

15. Sinclair, *The Flivver King* (Pasadena, 1937), p. 110.

16. Sinclair, *No Pasaran!* (Pasadena, 1937), p. 27.

17. Sinclair, *Little Steel* (Pasadena, 1938).

Chapter Ten

1. As Jung noted later, Sinclair's eagerness to attack institutional Christianity's surrounding of Jesus with heathenish superstition revealed his unwillingness to accept mysterious, inscrutable aspects of experience and human nature. C. G. Jung, "The Challenge of the Christian Enigma," *New Republic*, 128 (27 April 1953), 18–19. Even Sinclair's interest in psychic phenomena was founded on what he thought had been or could be empirically verified.

2. Sinclair, *Autobiography*, p. 292.

3. Sinclair, *O Shepherd, Speak* (New York, 1949), p. 583. The quoted passage is taken from an appended statement which was originally published in a 1940 Literary Guild bulletin.

4. *Ibid.*

5. *Ibid.*, p. 584.

6. Sinclair, *World's End* (New York, 1941), p. 483.

7. Sinclair's career long dependence on a conspiratorial understanding of history is well explained in Fretz, "Upton Sinclair: The Don Quixote of American Reform."

8. Sinclair, *Presidential Agent* (New York, 1944), p. 655.

9. Maxwell Geismar, "Lanny Budd on Another Secret Mission," *Saturday Review of Literature* (28 Aug. 1946) p. 13.

10. *Ibid.*

11. Earl N. Lockard, "Technique in the Novels of Upton Sinclair," diss. Chicago 1947, p. 95.

Chapter Eleven

1. These significant books do not include a short novel entitled *The Enemy Had It Too* (1950) dealing speculatively and topically but not compellingly with the development and potential future use of the atomic bomb.

2. Sinclair, "On Waldo Frank" (a letter to the editor), *Nation* (3 June 1953), p. 2. Sinclair wrote, "Communism is embodied for us by Malenkov, who has some fifteen millions of his political opponents in slave-labor camps and has murdered God alone knows how many more. The worst of anti-communism is typified to us by Senator McCarthy, who has lied recklessly about his political opponents, but has not been able to jail anybody, and has not murdered anybody so far as the record shows."

3. Sinclair, "Mr. Sinclair Inquires" (letter) *Nation* (4 Jan. 1965), back cover.

4. Sinclair, *Autobiography,* p. 312.

5. Robert Halsband, "Temptations of a Poor Country Maid," *Saturday Review of Literature* (29 April 1950), p. 9.

6. Sinclair, *Another Pamela, or Virtue Still Rewarded* (New York, 1950), p. 85.

7. Sinclair, *Affectionately, Eve* (New York, 1961).

8. There is considerable evidence that Sinclair not only based *Affectionately, Eve* on the life of Mary Craig Sinclair, but that he also wrote her autobiography. See Harris, *Upton Sinclair: American Rebel,* pp. 348–49.

9. Sinclair, *It Happened to Didymus* (New York, 1958), p. 57. This 1958 version is identical to *What Didymus Did* (London, 1954).

10. Sinclair, *Autobiography,* p. 329.

Chapter Twelve

1. Robert Cantwell, "Upton Sinclair," *After the Genteel Tradition,* ed. Malcolm Cowley (New York, 1937), pp. 37–51.

2. I am suggesting here that Sinclair could fit into the interpretation of Progressivism offered by David Noble in *The Paradox of Progressive Thought* (Minneapolis, 1958).

3. Justin Kaplan, *Lincoln Steffens: A Biography* (New York, 1974).

4. Fretz, "Upton Sinclair: The Don Quixote of American Reform."

5. F. Scott Fitzgerald, "My Generation," *Esquire: The Best of Forty Years,* compiled by the editors of *Esquire* (New York, 1973), p. 5.

6. Harris, *Upton Sinclair: American Rebel,* p. 3.

7. *Ibid.,* p. 4.

8. *Ibid.*

Selected Bibliography

Fortunately, Ronald Gottesman's *Upton Sinclair: An Annotated Checklist* (Kent: Kent State Univ. Press, 1973) is available to scholars interested in Sinclair. This bibliographical collection, the result of more than a decade of research, lists all of the publications by Sinclair from 1894 to 1967, translations and foreign editions of his works, published and unpublished works on Sinclair, reviews, and other useful information.

Serious scholars should also be aware of the extensive Sinclair material held by the Lilly Library of Indiana University. Before his death Sinclair deposited there literally thousands of publications, manuscripts, and letters that he had carefully kept for more than half a century.

The following pages list only major Sinclair books and useful secondary works. Sinclair's own works are in chronological order, with annotations as necessary. The secondary sources are in alphabetical order in two categories and are accompanied by explanatory remarks concerning their focus and usefulness.

PRIMARY SOURCES

Springtime and Harvest: A Romance. New York: Sinclair Press, 1901.
    Reissued as *King Midas: A Romance* by Funk & Wagnalls later in 1901.
The Journal of Arthur Stirling. New York: D. Appleton, 1903.
Prince Hagen. Boston: L. C. Page, 1903.
Manassas. New York: Macmillan, 1904.
The Jungle. New York: Doubleday, Page, 1906.
A Captain of Industry. Girard, Kansas: *Appeal to Reason*, 1906. Written 1902–1903.
The Industrial Republic. New York: Doubleday, Page, 1907.
The Overman. New York: Doubleday, Page, 1907. Written 1902–1903.
The Metropolis. New York: Moffat, Yard, 1908.
The Moneychangers. New York: B. W. Dodge, 1908.
Samuel the Seeker. New York: B. W. Dodge, 1910.
Love's Pilgrimage. New York: Mitchell Kennerley, 1911.
Plays of Protest. New York: Mitchell Kennerley, 1912. Includes "The

169

Naturewoman," "The Machine," "The Second-Story Man," "Prince Hagen."

Sylvia. Philadelphia: John C. Winston, 1913.

Sylvia's Marriage. Philadelphia: John C. Winston, 1914.

King Coal. New York: Macmillan, 1917.

The Profits of Religion. Pasadena: Sinclair, 1918.

Jimmie Higgins. New York: Boni and Liveright; Pasadena: Sinclair, 1919.

The Brass Check. Pasadena: Sinclair, 1920.

100%: The Story of a Patriot. Pasadena: Sinclair, 1920.

The Book of Life. Pasadena: Sinclair-Paine, 1922.

They Call Me Carpenter. Pasadena: Sinclair; New York: Boni and Liveright, 1922.

The Goose-Step: A Study of American Education. Pasadena: Sinclair, 1923.

The Goslings. Pasadena: Sinclair, 1924.

The Millennium: A Comedy of the Year 2000. Pasadena: Sinclair, 1924. Originally published as a serial in 1914.

Singing Jailbirds: A Drama in Four Acts. Pasadena: Sinclair, 1924.

Mammonart. Pasadena: Sinclair, 1925.

Oil! New York: A. & C. Boni; Long Beach: Sinclair, 1927.

Money Writes! New York: A. & C. Boni; Long Beach: Sinclair, 1927.

Boston. New York: A. & C. Boni; Pasadena: Sinclair, 1928.

Mountain City. New York: A. & C. Boni; Long Beach: Sinclair, 1930.

Roman Holiday. New York: Farrar and Rinehart; Pasadena: Sinclair, 1931.

The Wet Parade. New York: Farrar and Rinehart; Pasadena: Sinclair, 1931.

American Outpost. New York: Farrar and Rinehart; Pasadena: Sinclair, 1932.

I, Governor of California, and How I Ended Poverty. Los Angeles: Sinclair; New York: Farrar and Rinehart, 1933.

Upton Sinclair Presents William Fox. Los Angeles: Sinclair, 1933.

Co-Op: A Novel of Living Together. New York: Farrar and Rinehart; Pasadena: Sinclair, 1936.

What God Means to Me: An Attempt at a Working Religion. New York: Farrar and Rinehart; Pasadena: Sinclair, 1936.

The Flivver King. Pasadena: Sinclair, 1937.

No Pasaran! Pasadena: Sinclair, 1937.

Little Steel. New York: Farrar and Rinehart; Pasadena: Sinclair, 1938.

Our Lady. Pasadena: Sinclair, 1938.

Terror in Russia? Two Views. New York: Richard R. Smith, 1938. With Eugene Lyons.

Marie Antoinette. New York: Vanguard Press; Pasadena: Sinclair, 1939.

World's End. New York: Viking Press, 1940.

Between Two Worlds. New York: Viking Press, 1941.

Dragon's Teeth. New York: Viking Press, 1942.

Wide Is the Gate. New York: Viking Press, 1943.

Presidential Agent. New York: Viking Press, 1944.

Dragon Harvest. New York: Viking Press, 1945.
A World to Win. New York: Viking Press, 1946.
Presidential Mission. New York: Viking Press, 1947.
One Clear Call. New York: Viking Press, 1948.
O Shepherd, Speak! New York: Viking Press, 1948.
Another Pamela: or Virtue Still Rewarded. New York: Viking Press, 1950.
A Personal Jesus: Portrait and Interpretation. New York: Evans Publishing
    Co., 1952.
The Return of Lanny Budd. New York: Viking Press, 1953.
What Didymus Did. London: Allan Wingate, 1954. Published in the United
    States in 1958 as *It Happened to Didymus*, by the Sagamore Press.
My Lifetime in Letters. Columbia: Univ. of Missouri Press, 1962. A collection
    chosen and arranged by Sinclair.
Affectionately, Eve. New York: Twayne Publishers, 1961.
The Autobiography of Upton Sinclair. New York: Harcourt, Brace & World,
    1962.

SECONDARY SOURCES

1. General Studies

AARON, DANIEL. *Writers on the Left*. New York: Avon Books. Covers
    American radical writers from 1910 to World War II, with particular
    emphasis on their contact with Communism.
BLOTNER, JOSEPH. *The Modern American Political Novel*. Austin: Univ.
    of Texas Press, 1966. Useful for its examination of economic themes
    in works by major American writers, not including Sinclair.
FILLER, LOUIS. *The Muckrakers: Crusaders for American Liberalism*.
    Chicago: Henry Regnery, 1968. A standard study of muckraking as a
    phenomenon of American journalism and literature, with considera-
    ble attention to Sinclair.
HOFFMAN, FREDERICK J. *The Twenties: American Writing in the Postwar
    Decade*, rev. ed. New York: Free Press, 1962. Imperative for
    understanding the context and variety of American expression in the
    twenties.
JONES, HOWARD MUMFORD. *The Age of Energy: Varieties of American
    Experience, 1865–1914*. New York: Viking, 1971. A thorough
    cultural history of the period.
KAZIN, ALFRED. *On Native Grounds*. New York, Doubleday, 1955. An
    examination of American prose writing from the 1890s to World War
    II.
LYNN, KENNETH S. *The Dream of Success*. Boston: Little, Brown, 1955.
    Analyzes several of Sinclair's important contemporaries in the terms
    of their desire for success.

MARTIN, JAY. *Harvests of Change: American Literature, 1865–1914*. A comprehensive study of the responses of American writers during this period to their social and cultural context.

MILLGATE, MICHAEL. *American Social Fiction*. New York: Barnes and Noble, 1964. Focuses on major American novels and briefly treats several works by Sinclair.

RIDEOUT, WALTER B. *The Radical Novel in the United States*. New York: Hill and Wang, 1956. Comprehensively and perceptibly analyzes radical fiction in twentieth century American literature.

WIEBE, ROBERT H. *The Search for Order, 1877–1920*. New York: Hill and Wang, 1967. Provides an understanding of the social and political context of Sinclair's early career.

2. Studies of Sinclair or His Works.

BIELLA, ARNOLD P. "Upton Sinclair: Crusader." Ph.D. diss., Stanford, 1954. Provides a sympathetic interpretation of Sinclair's efforts in the cause of social justice.

BLOODWORTH, WILLIAM A., JR. "The Early Years of Upton Sinclair: The Making of a Progressive Christian Socialist." Ph.D. diss., Texas, 1972. Interprets Sinclair's career up through *The Jungle* from a psychological and historical perspective.

BROOKS, VAN WYCK. *Emerson and Others*. New York: E. P. Dutton, 1927, pp. 209–217. Assesses Sinclair's novels as rhetorically weak.

CANTWELL, ROBERT. "Upton Sinclair." In *After the Genteel Tradition*, ed. Malcolm Cowley. New York: Norton, 1937. Makes a strong case for Sinclair as an important figure in modern American literature.

DELL, FLOYD. *Upton Sinclair: A Study in Social Protest*. New York: George H. Doran, 1927. Offers a balanced, sympathetic view of Sinclair by a leading literary figure of the twenties.

FOLSOM, MICHAEL B. "Literary Radicalism and Genteel Tradition: A Study of the Principal Literary Works of the American Socialist Movement Before 1912." Ph.D. diss., California, 1972. Includes a long and incisive chapter on *The Jungle*.

FRETZ, LEWIS A. "Upton Sinclair: The Don Quixote of American Reform." Ph.D. diss., Stanford, 1970. Offers an intelligent but highly critical analysis of Sinclair's political thought.

GOTTESMAN, RONALD. "Upton Sinclair: An Annotated Bibliographical Catalogue, 1894–1932." Ph.D. diss., Indiana, 1964. Provides a narrative of Sinclair's early career as well as bibliographical information.

HARRIS, LEON. *Upton Sinclair: American Rebel*. New York: Thomas Y. Crowell, 1975. Provides a thorough account of Sinclair's life and illuminates the emotional divisions behind much of his career.

MORDELL, ALBERT. *Haldeman-Julius and Upton Sinclair: The Amazing Record of a Long Collaboration*. Girard, Kansas: Haldeman-Julius,

1950. Traces Sinclair's relationship with the populist publisher and provides much information about Sinclair's interest in psychic phenomena.

SWADOS, HARVEY. "The World of Upton Sinclair," *Atlantic Monthly,* Dec. 1961, pp. 96–102. Favorably assesses *The Jungle* as an important historical document and as an effective piece of propaganda in 1906.

YODER, JON. *Upton Sinclair.* New York: Ungar, 1975. Provides a good, though brief, survey of Sinclair's career and his major works.

Index

174